curry everyday

*Over 100 simple
vegetarian recipes
from Jaipur to Japan*

I would like to dedicate this book to my wife Deepti and my children, Amisha and Arjun.

Their formidable support has propelled me to the position I am in today. It's truly a privilege to be a husband and father to this family.

curry everyday

Over 100 simple vegetarian recipes from Jaipur to Japan

atul kochhar

with photography by Mike Cooper

BLOOMSBURY ABSOLUTE

LONDON · OXFORD · NEW YORK · NEW DELHI · SYDNEY

ontents

intr

oduction

For me, curry isn't a term that defines a dish, but, as celebrated Chinese-American chef Ken Hom says, 'is a term that refers to a style of cookery and not a single taste or degree of spiciness', and that was the basis on which I gathered recipes for this book. Every recipe in these pages is linked loosely by technique and style, ingredients that crop up across countries and continents, and, of course, by deliciousness, too.

In India, a curry traditionally refers to a spiced dish with a sauce, gravy or masala base. Over the years, as the world has opened up through travel, trade, relationships and interaction between countries, Indian cuisine has changed as a direct result of sharing cultures, and, most importantly, ingredients. Through these cultural exchanges, Indian food has, in my opinion, been enriched. In turn, other nations have borrowed from our customs and created curry dishes of their own, many of which have been collected here for you; a trip around the world through curry recipes. You can say that in this cultural exchange, the best bits from various cuisines and cultures have been brought together, and ultimately this book is a celebration of those glorious recipes.

It is only natural that neighbouring countries might have similar approaches to food, and recipes can seem fairly fluid between them. For example, the aromatics used in recipes across Southeast Asia tend to have a common thread, while Malaysian and Indonesian curries have a heavy focus on chillies, coconut and curry leaves. Each country or region has its own rich and complex subtleties; a different focus on sweet, sour and spicy notes, for example. Indeed, as recipes travel, cooks adapt the original and make their own versions more in line with their cuisine or local produce. For example, lentil recipes from different countries might use the same variety of lentils, but the other ingredients and techniques used in their preparation may change. Indeed, from Ethiopia to the UAE and South Africa to Pakistan, the variations are so clear.

In the research and recipe development for this book, I learnt new techniques such as how to make the spicy coriander-chilli sauce *zhoug* (page 248), and experimented with new flavours, including brown jasmine rice (page 283). I love that even after all these years, I am still learning in the kitchen, and enjoying different cuisines and ingredients as much as ever.

In the introduction of *Curries of the World*, I explained in detail how even within India there's huge variation in spices and ingredients from north to south, and this is magnified when viewing curries on a global scale. Of course, geography and regional produce plays a huge part in what we eat, and within this book I've often substituted ingredients more easily available in the UK than they are in Thailand or Malaysia, for example, but without compromising on the basis of the recipe, and the authentic spices.

On the whole, I think it's fair to say that people are now consuming less meat, so it was important to me that this book would be purely vegetarian, and indeed many of the recipes are vegan, too. Among friends and customers at my restaurants, the last few years have marked a definite change in how people eat; we are all becoming much more conscious of the provenance of ingredients, and the impact our food is having on the environment. As a result, I have increased the number of vegetarian and vegan dishes on our a la carte menus, as well as creating vegan and vegetarian tasting menus at most of my restaurants. It's encouraged me and my chefs to get creative, to explore traditional flavours but with different ingredients, and to share these vegetarian dishes with our guests. Gone are the days of a disappointing nut roast or over-baked stuffed mushrooms, as vegetarian food takes on a new life and is celebrated in home kitchens and restaurant dining rooms. A few of particular favourite dishes are Moroccan Chermoula Cauliflower (page 88), Yemeni Spicy Potato Stew (page 92), and Singaporean Curried Mango (page 79). Inspired by experiments for this book, some of the recipes have made in on to the menus of my restaurants, too.

Many countries included in this book have always had a more vegetable-led diet than we have in the west, mostly because of the expense and lack of availability of meat. Many of the recipes in these pages are naturally vegetarian, such as Sri Lankan Red Lentil Curry with Spinach (page 202), or Pakistan's Mixed Vegetable Curry (page 218), Nepal's Stir-fried Mustard Greens (page 183) and Tunisia's Chickpea Soup with Fried Eggs (page 84). Others have been adapted from a traditional meat-based recipe to make them vegetarian or vegan, such as the South African Bobotie (page 128), which is usually made with lamb; both versions are delicious.

I wanted this book to be a reflection of the way we eat now and enjoy food socially, so many of the recipes are designed for sharing and mixing and matching, making them perfect for feeding a crowd. Obviously, recipes from within countries will work well together, but try a global feast with

Spiced Red Lentil Stew (page 106) from Ethiopia and Pickled Potatoes (page 182) from Nepal, paired with Aubergine & Tofu Katsu Curry (page 56) from Japan for a really great dinner. Beyond that, the majority of these recipes can be made as a main course and I've suggested accompaniments, such as naans, parathas or rice. I've given my recipes for these (pages 283–293), but, of course, the choice is yours.

The basis for many of the recipes in this book are the curry and spice powders and pastes (pages 270–281), and it is these that will bring that authentic flavour to each recipe. The different combinations of spices used in various parts of the world will unravel as you experiment with the recipes and work your way around the world, so enjoy the adventure.

Some of these pastes and powders might seem like they make individual recipes more complicated, but they will make such a difference to your cooking, and once made they're easy to store so you'll have them to hand for quick mid-week suppers, or for jazzing up roasted vegetables or salads.

And finally, don't forget to make the best use of your freezer – fresh herbs, lime leaves, chillies, lemongrass and spice pastes can all be kept in the freezer, reducing waste and extending shelf life.

I hope you enjoy eating your way around the world with these delicious curries – happy cooking!

Atul Kochhar,
London

far

east asia

This simple, straightforward recipe has a lovely smoky flavour from the paprika and subtle heat from the fermented chilli paste. Even my teenage son – not always easy to please – pronounced this good enough to have a second helping. I serve this spooned over freshly boiled sticky rice (page 284) with a selection of stir-fried vegetables. Asian pickles alongside are a great accompaniment.

Sweet Potato Curry
goguma kale (kare)

1½ tablespoons sunflower oil
1 large onion, finely chopped
3 garlic cloves, finely chopped
1.5cm piece fresh galangal or
    ginger, peeled and chopped
4 sweet potatoes or about 600g
    butternut squash, peeled and
    cut into bite-sized cubes
½ teaspoon smoked paprika
400ml coconut milk
300ml vegetable stock, ideally
    home-made (page 282)
1 teaspoon rice wine vinegar
1½ teaspoons runny honey
1 tablespoon Korean fermented
    chilli paste (*gochujang*)
1 teaspoon soy sauce
2 tablespoons unsalted skinned
    peanuts, coarsely crushed,
    to garnish
chopped coriander leaves,
    to garnish

Heat the oil in a wok over a high heat. Add the onion, garlic and galangal or ginger, and stir-fry until the onion is translucent. Add the sweet potatoes and paprika and keep stir-frying for 30 seconds to cook the paprika. Watch closely so nothing burns.

Stir in the coconut milk, vegetable stock, rice wine vinegar, honey, chilli paste and soy sauce, and bring to the boil. Reduce the heat a little and leave to simmer for 20 minutes, stirring occasionally, or until the sweet potatoes are tender. Taste and adjust the soy sauce and vinegar, if necessary. Garnish with peanuts and coriander and serve.

The title says it all – this example of Korean street food is hot and spicy. That's exactly how I like this, but I appreciate not everyone wants as much chilli, so add the chilli paste and flakes to suit your palate. You'll find rice cakes also labelled as rice sticks, and their mild flavour provides a perfect foil to the spiciness of the sauce. As they cook, they become soft, but remain quite chewy.

Hot & Spicy Rice Cakes
tteokbokki

600ml vegetable stock, ideally home-made (page 282)

125g shiitake mushrooms, trimmed and quartered or chopped

3 garlic cloves, finely chopped

1 carrot, peeled, halved lengthwise and very thinly sliced

1 spring onion, white and green parts sliced separately

¼ head Chinese cabbage, cored and finely shredded

3 tablespoons Korean fermented chilli paste (*gochujang*), or to taste

2 teaspoons tamari or soy sauce

1 teaspoon light brown sugar

½ teaspoon red chilli flakes, or to taste

450g rice cakes, separated into pieces

toasted sesame oil, to garnish

black and white sesame seeds, to garnish, optional

Pour the stock into a large, deep frying pan or saucepan with lid and bring to the boil. Stir in the mushrooms, garlic, carrot, the white part of the spring onion and the Chinese cabbage. Cover and return the liquid to the boil.

Uncover and stir in the chilli paste, tamari sauce, brown sugar and red chilli flakes, and return to the boil. Stir in the rice cakes, then re-cover the pan, reduce the heat and leave to simmer for about 10 minutes, until the rice cakes are very tender and plump. Stir occasionally so the rice sticks do not to stick to the bottom of the pan and add a splash of water, if necessary. Taste and adjust the amount of tamari sauce if necessary, and if you want more heat, stir in extra fermented chilli paste.

To serve, scatter over the reserved green part of the spring onion, drizzle with sesame oil and sprinkle with the black and white sesame seeds.

Left: Hot & Spicy Rice
Cakes (page 13)
Right: Twice-fried Spicy
Cauliflower (page 16)

Even in a professional kitchen I don't like to deep-fry.
I never have. In this recipe, however, it's necessary – the
first frying cooks the florets, and the second frying gives
them a crispier texture before they are added to the
spiced vegetable mixture – it has a real chilli kick from the
fermented chilli paste, a staple of every Korean kitchen.
There aren't many hard-and-fast rules with the vegetable
mixture. I've used red cabbage, red onion and spring
onions, but you could also use green or white cabbage
along with sliced leeks. For more variety, substitute
broccoli florets for the cauliflower.

Twice-fried Spicy Cauliflower
bokk-eun geos kolli peullawo

4 tablespoons cornflour
1 teaspoon garlic powder
1 large cauliflower, trimmed and
  cut into bite-sized florets
250ml vegetable stock, ideally
  home-made (page 282),
  plus extra 2 tablespoons for
  sprinkling over the cauliflower
¼ teaspoon red chilli powder
sunflower oil
1 garlic clove, finely chopped
70g red cabbage, cored and
  finely shredded
2 spring onions, trimmed and
  thinly sliced
1 carrot, peeled and finely diced
1 red onion, finely chopped
sea salt and freshly ground
  black pepper
toasted sesame oil, for drizzling
red chilli, finely sliced, to garnish
chopped coriander leaves, to
  garnish, optional
white sesame seeds, to garnish,
  optional

First make the sauce. Put all the sauce ingredients
in a bowl and mix together. Set aside.

Put the 4 tablespoons cornflour and the garlic
powder in a shallow bowl with salt and pepper to
taste, and stir together. Set aside. Put the cauliflower
florets in a separate bowl and sprinkle over 2
tablespoons vegetable stock to slightly moisten
them. Add the chilli powder with salt to taste and
use your hands to mix everything together.

Heat enough sunflower oil for deep-frying in a deep-
fat fryer or heavy-based saucepan until it reaches
175°C. Line a large plate with a double layer of
kitchen paper.

Meanwhile, toss the cauliflower florets in the
cornflour mixture, then add as many florets as will
fit in the pan without overcrowding and deep-fry,
stirring, for about 1 minute until light golden brown.
Use a slotted spoon to transfer to the paper-lined
plate to drain. Cook in batches and reheat the oil
between batches, if necessary. Set the pan of oil
aside.

For the sauce

1½ tablespoons vegetable
stock, ideally home-made
(page 282)
2 teaspoons soy sauce
1 teaspoon Korean fermented
chilli paste (*gochujang*)
1 teaspoon vegetarian
oyster sauce
1 teaspoon light brown sugar
½ teaspoon cornflour
½ teaspoon prepared mustard

Heat a large wok over a medium-high heat. Add 2 tablespoons oil and swirl it around. Add the garlic and stir to flavour the oil. Add the cabbage, spring onions, carrot and red onion, and stir-fry until the vegetables begin to soften.

Add 250ml vegetable stock, bring to the boil and leave it to bubble away until the vegetables are softened and the liquid is reduced by half. Stir in the prepared sauce and continue boiling until the carrot is tender. Leave to simmer while you fry the florets a second time.

Reheat the oil to 175°C. Add the cauliflower florets and fry for just a few seconds to crisp them. Use a slotted spoon to transfer them to the vegetable mixture as they turn a darker golden brown. Work quickly so they do not burn.

Stir everything together, taste and adjust the salt, if necessary. Drizzle with sesame oil and garnish with the red chilli, chopped coriander and sesame seeds, if using. It's ready to serve.

This traditional recipe, dating from the 16th century, is a fusion of Malay and Chinese cooking. Numerous legends exist about how this rich coconut curry was developed, but one explanation is that a local Malay cook created it for a Chinese ship's captain, or '*kapitan*'. Serve this with plenty of jasmine rice (page 283).

Captian's Curry
kari kapitan

2 teaspoons groundnut or
  sunflower oil
2.5cm piece of cinnamon bark
400g plant-based 'chicken'
  pieces
400ml coconut milk
200ml vegetable stock, ideally
  home-made (page 282)
1 tablespoon grated jaggery or
  Demerara sugar
1 tablespoon tamarind extract
  (see Atul's tip, page 167)
sea salt and black pepper
coriander sprigs, to garnish
1 small red onion, thinly sliced,
  to garnish, optional

For the curry paste
3 dried red chillies, soaked in hot
  water for at least 20 minutes
1.5cm piece of galangal or fresh
  ginger, peeled and chopped
1cm piece of fresh turmeric,
  peeled and chopped, or
  ½ teaspoon ground turmeric
6 shallots, chopped
5 garlic cloves, chopped
2 teaspoons Chinese five-spice
  powder
½ teaspoon vegetarian fish sauce
½ teaspoon sea salt

First, make the curry paste. Drain the chillies and remove the stem ends. Put them and the remaining paste ingredients in a food processor and process until a semi-smooth sauce forms, scraping down the side of the bowl as necessary. Alternatively, pound the ingredients together with a pestle and mortar. Set aside.

Heat a large wok over a high heat. Add the oil and swirl it around. Add the curry paste with the cinnamon bark and stir-fry for 1 minute to cook the spices in the paste. It should be very fragrant at this point.

Reduce the heat to low and add the 'chicken' pieces, stirring to coat them with the curry paste. Pour in the coconut milk and stock, then stir in the sugar, tamarind extract and salt and pepper to taste. Bring to the boil, then reduce the heat to low and leave to simmer for a couple of minutes until the 'chicken' pieces are hot.

Stir in the coriander, taste and adjust the salt and pepper, if necessary. Garnish with red onion slices, if using, and serve.

18   curry everyday   **far east asia**

Jackfruit grows wild in Malaysia, so it gets used in all kinds of savoury and sweet dishes. I first encountered this substantial curry, with its puréed cashew nuts for richness and creaminess, on a television filming trip, and I was determined to recreate a recipe. I serve this with basmati rice (page 283), jasmine rice (page 283) or chapatis (page 288), followed by a selection of fresh fruit.

Jackfruit & Aubergine Curry

nyonya dan terung kari

100g unsalted cashew nuts, soaked for 1 hour in water to cover

sunflower oil or ghee

200g firm tofu, patted dry and cut into bite-sized pieces

2 tablespoons Malay Curry Powder (page 274)

1 teaspoon cornflour

1 can (400g) jackfruit pieces, drained and patted dry

10cm piece of cinnamon bark

4 shallots, finely chopped

1 tablespoon Ginger-Garlic Paste (page 281)

red chilli powder, to taste

150g aubergine, cut into bite-sized pieces

a large pinch of saffron threads, soaked in 4 tablespoons water

250g full-fat natural yogurt

2 tomatoes, chopped

sea salt

chopped coriander, to garnish, optional

Drain the cashew nuts, then pat them dry. Transfer them to a food processor and process until a paste forms. Set aside.

Heat a wok over a medium heat. Add 2 tablespoons oil and swirl it around. Add the tofu and fry, using tongs to turn the pieces, until they are coloured all over. Remove from the wok using a slotted spoon and set aside.

Mix together 2 teaspoons of the curry powder, the cornflour and a pinch of salt. Toss the jackfruit pieces with this mixture until they are well coated. Reheat the wok over a high heat. Add enough extra oil to the wok to make a thin layer. Add as many jackfruit pieces as will fit without overcrowding and shallow-fry, using tongs to turn, until coloured and slightly crisp. Set aside and continue with the rest of the jackfruit until all the pieces are fried. Set aside.

Reheat the washed and dried wok over a high heat. Add 2 tablespoons oil and swirl around. Reduce the heat, add the cinnamon bark and shallots and stir-fry until the shallots turn translucent. Add the ginger-garlic paste, red chilli powder, cashew paste and the remaining curry powder, and continue stir-frying for 1 minute. Make sure the ginger and garlic get cooked at this point, but watch closely that the ground spices don't burn.

Add the aubergine to the wok with salt to taste and stir so it is well coated with the mixture. Add the saffron threads and their soaking liquid and enough water to just cover all the ingredients. Bring to the boil, stirring, then reduce the heat and leave to simmer for 20 minutes, or until the aubergine is tender. Add a little extra water, if the mixture looks like it is becoming too dry.

Stir in the yogurt, tomatoes, fried tofu and jackfruit pieces, and continue simmering for about 5 minutes until the tomatoes are breaking down. Taste and adjust the salt, if necessary. Garnish and serve.

Top: Tofu Curry (page 24)
Left: Jackfruit & Choi Sum
Nyonya Curry (page 25)
Right: 'Chicken' Laksa, Kuala
Lumpur Style (page 26)

Malay kormas differ from the Indian version in that they contain star anise, so this has a slightly different flavour than I am most familiar with. There is a strong Indian influence in Malay cooking, as a large Indian population emigrated, especially from the Tamil Nadu region, to Malaysia during the time of British rule, taking their culture and cuisine with them.

Tofu Curry
tofu kurma kari

2 tablespoons groundnut or
  sunflower oil
6 shallots, thinly sliced
4 garlic cloves, finely chopped
2 fresh red chillies, thinly sliced
1 teaspoon ground turmeric
2 star anise
3cm piece of fresh galangal
  or fresh ginger, peeled and
  finely chopped
seeds from 4 green
  cardamom pods
2 tablespoons Malaysian Kurma
  Powder (page 274)
400ml coconut milk
400ml vegetable stock, ideally
  home-made (page 282)
1 teaspoon vegetarian fish sauce
600g firm tofu, patted dry, or
  tempeh, cut into bite-sized
  pieces
150g mangetout
freshly squeezed lime juice,
  to taste
sea salt
chopped coriander leaves,
  to garnish, optional
toasted sesame oil, to drizzle

Heat a wok over a medium-high heat. Add the oil and swirl it around. Add the shallots and garlic with a pinch of salt and stir-fry until the shallots are translucent. Add the red chillies, turmeric, star anise, galangal and cardamom seeds, and continue stir-frying for 1 minute to cook the garlic and galangal. Lower the heat and add the curry powder and stir-fry for 30 seconds. Watch closely so none of the ingredients burn.

Add the coconut milk, stock and fish sauce, and bring to the boil, stirring. Reduce the heat to medium and leave the sauce to simmer for about 5 minutes for the flavours to blend.

Add the tofu and mangetout and continue simmering until they are hot and the mangetout is tender, but still with some bite. Stir in the lime juice and adjust the salt, if necessary. Serve, garnished with coriander leaves, if using, and sesame oil drizzled over.

Serves 4

A Nyonya recipe comes from the unique cooking style of Chinese-Malay families known as the Peranakans. Descendants of early Chinese settlers in Malacca, Penang and Singapore, their culinary repertoire combines traditional Chinese ingredients with local herbs and seasonings, such as the lemongrass and turmeric here.

Jackfruit & Choi Sum Nyonya Curry
nyonya dan choi sum

4 tablespoons groundnut oil
4 or 5 fresh or freeze-dried Makrut lime leaves, fine central ribs removed
1 lemongrass stalk, outer layers removed and the stalk bashed
4 tablespoons tamarind water (see Atul's tip, page 167)
1½ teaspoons palm or light brown sugar
1 teaspoon ground coriander
½ teaspoon ground turmeric
200ml water
400ml coconut milk
4–6 cherry tomatoes
1 can (400g) jackfruit pieces, drained
200g choi sum, stalks and leaves separated, chopped and rinsed
150g bean sprouts
sea salt
coriander leaves, to garnish

For the curry paste
2 dried red chillies, soaked in hot water for at least 20 minutes
2.5cm piece of fresh galangal, peeled and chopped
3 garlic cloves, peeled
1 lemongrass stalk, outer layers removed and the stalk bashed
1 onion, chopped

First, make the curry paste. Strain the chillies, reserving the soaking water, and remove the stem ends. Transfer the chillies to a food processor with the galangal, garlic, lemongrass and onion, and process until a fine paste forms, scraping down the side of the bowl as necessary, and adding a few tablespoons of the soaking water to break down the ingredients to make a smooth paste.

Heat a large wok over a high heat. Add the oil and swirl it around. Reduce the heat slightly, add the spice paste and stir-fry until it is aromatic. Stand back when you add the paste to the hot wok, because the moisture in the paste will make it splatter.

Add the Makrut lime leaves, lemongrass, tamarind water, sugar, ground coriander and turmeric with salt to taste, and continue stir-frying for 3–4 minutes until the fat separates from the paste. Gradually stir in the 200ml water to keep the mixture moist and prevent it from burning.

Stir in the coconut milk, cherry tomatoes, jackfruit pieces and choi sum stalks, and bring to the boil, stirring. Lower the heat and leave to simmer, stirring occasionally, for about 5 minutes until the tomatoes and jackfruit pieces are hot and the choi sum stalks are almost tender. Add the choi sum leaves and continue simmering until they wilt and the stalks are tender. Stir in the bean sprouts. Adjust the salt, if necessary, garnish with coriander and serve.

When most people think of Malay food, I think there is a good chance laksa comes to mind – this fragrant bowl of semi-thick coconut soup with 'chicken' pieces, pan-fried tofu and fresh egg noodles truly is a meal in bowl. Freshly squeezed lime juice and chillies are added at the end for an extra flavour zing.

'Chicken' Laksa, Kuala Lumpur Style
laksa

2 tablespoons cornflour
100g firm tofu, patted dry and
   cut into bite-sized pieces
groundnut or sunflower oil
2.5cm piece of cinnamon bark
400g plant-based 'chicken'
   pieces or Quorn
2 lemongrass stalks, outer layers
   removed and the stalks bashed
400ml coconut milk
200ml vegetable stock, ideally
   home-made (page 282),
   or water
2 teaspoons palm sugar or light
   brown sugar
200g bean sprouts, rinsed
200g precooked Chinese egg
   noodles, soaked in hot water
   to cover, to soften
2 tablespoons chopped
   coriander leaves and stalks
sea salt

For the spice paste
8–10 black peppercorns, to taste
2 small dried red chillies, stem
   ends removed
1 clove
3 tablespoons coriander seeds
1 teaspoon cumin seeds
1 teaspoon fennel seeds
¼ teaspoon ground turmeric

First, make the spice paste. Put the peppercorns, dried red chillies, clove, coriander seeds, cumin seeds, fennel seeds and ground turmeric in a food processor, and process until a fine powder forms. Add the water, shallots and fish sauce, and continue processing to make a fine paste, scraping down the side of the bowl as necessary. Set aside.

Next, shallow-fry the tofu. Put the cornflour in a shallow bowl. Add the tofu, a few pieces at a time, and toss until they are coated, then tap off any excess and set aside. Repeat until all pieces are coated. Line a plate with kitchen paper and set aside.

Heat a thin layer of oil in a wok over a medium-high heat. Add as many tofu pieces as will fit without overcrowding and fry, using tongs to turn the pieces, until lightly coloured all over. Transfer to the lined plate and set aside. Continue until all the tofu is fried, adding a little more oil to the pan, as necessary. Stand well back when you add the tofu because, even if it has been well pressed, the water in it will splatter in the hot oil.

Re-heat the washed and dried wok over a high heat. Add 3 tablespoons oil and swirl around. Reduce the heat to medium, add the cinnamon bark and spice paste and stir-fry for 8–10 minutes to cook out the rawness from the shallots. It should smell aromatic at this point. Watch closely to make sure the paste doesn't burn. If you think it's starting to catch, stir in a little water.

100ml water
5 shallots, coarsely chopped
1 teaspoon vegetarian fish sauce

To garnish
1 large fresh red chilli, sliced on
   the diagonal
coriander and mint sprigs, finely
   shredded, optional
1 lime, quartered
fried onions

Add the 'chicken' pieces and lemongrass stalks and gently stir into the paste, taking care not to break up the 'chicken' pieces. Stir in the coconut milk, vegetable stock, palm sugar and salt to taste, and bring to the boil. Reduce the heat and leave to simmer for 10 minutes, or until the 'chicken' is hot and the flavours blended. Add the tofu, increase the heat and leave to simmer for 1 or 2 minutes until the tofu is hot.

Meanwhile, bring a saucepan of water to the boil. Add the bean sprouts and quickly blanch. Drain and rinse under cold running water – you want them to retain some crunch, but not be completely raw. Transfer the bean sprouts to 4 large bowls. Drain the noodles and add them to the bowls.

Stir the coriander leaves and stalks into the soup, taste and adjust the salt, if necessary. Use a slotted spoon to divide the 'chicken' pieces and tofu among the bowls, then ladle over the coconut soup. Garnish each bowl with red chilli slices, coriander and mint sprigs, if using, and a lime quarter for squeezing over. Sprinkle over the fried onions and serve. Leave the lemongrass behind in the wok.

Jackfruit doesn't have a lot of flavour, which is why I marinate it in a well-balanced satay paste before cooking. My version has the sourness of tamarind and sweetness from sugar and sweet soy sauce to balance the heat from the chillies. There is a lot of preparation with this recipe, but it can all be done in advance and the actual cooking is quick and easy. I've given you the option of grilling or barbecuing the skewers, but I like these best cooked on a barbecue – satays really come alive when cooked over charcoal.

Jackfruit Satay
nongka saté

2 x 400g cans jackfruit pieces, drained
sunflower oil for greasing

For the Indonesian satay paste
4 or 5 fresh red chillies, to taste, chopped
4 garlic cloves, chopped
4 shallots, chopped
2 fresh or freeze-dried Makrut lime leaves, fine central ribs removed
1.5cm piece fresh galangal or ginger, peeled and chopped
6 tablespoons sunflower oil
4 tablespoons tamarind water (see Atul's tip, page 167)
2 tablespoons sweet soy sauce (*kecap manis*)

To serve (optional)
1 lime, quartered
spring onions, finely chopped
mint leaves, chopped
Peanut Dipping Sauce (page 291)

If using bamboo or wooden skewers, put 8 skewers in a bowl of water and leave to soak for at least 1 hour. Transfer to a bowl and set aside.

Meanwhile, make the spice paste. Put all the paste ingredients in a food processor and process until a fine paste forms, scraping down the side of the bowl as necessary. Alternatively, pound the ingredients together with a pestle and mortar.

Put the spice paste a large bowl, add the jackfruit pieces and stir together gently so they are well coated. Cover and chill in the fridge for at least 15 minutes, or up to 6 hours.

Just before you are ready to cook, light a charcoal barbecue and leave until the coals are glowing, or preheat a grill to high and line the grill pan with aluminium foil.

Gently thread the jackfruit pieces on to the skewers. Brush the barbecue grid or grill rack with oil, then add the skewers and grill for 3–4 minutes, turning so they lightly browned all over. Transfer to a platter and squeeze over fresh lime juice, then serve with lime wedges, spring onions and mint leaves, if using. Give each person a portion of the peanut dipping sauce.

Sayurs are popular throughout Indonesia, both as street food and in homes and restaurants. Whatever the main ingredients, it will always contain a mix of seasonal vegetables swimming in coconut curry, like a thin stew. I serve with a simple stir-fried vegetable, rice or flatbread.

Vegetable & Tofu Coconut Stew
sayur lodeh

sunflower oil
400g firm tofu, patted dry and
    cut into bite-sized pieces
¾ teaspoon mild curry powder
    of your choice
100g aubergine, sliced and
    quartered
100g Chinese napa cabbage,
    chopped
100g green beans, trimmed and
    halved or quartered
50g carrots, peeled and thinly
    sliced
800ml coconut milk
1 teaspoon palm or light brown
    sugar, or to taste
1 lime, halved
sea salt

For the curry paste
5cm piece of fresh turmeric,
    peeled and chopped, or
    1 teaspoon ground turmeric
25g piece of fresh galangal,
    peeled and chopped
6 candlenuts or macadamia nuts,
    chopped
2 dried red chillies, chopped
2 lemongrass stalks, outer layers
    removed and the stalks bashed
    and chopped
1 tablespoon bottled chilli-garlic
    sauce

First, make the curry paste. Put all the paste ingredients in a spice grinder or coffee grinder with 2 tablespoons water and process until a fine paste forms, scraping down the side of the bowl or grinder, as necessary. Alternatively, use a pestle and mortar. Set aside.

Heat a large wok over a high heat. Add enough oil to make a thin layer and swirl it around. Add as many tofu pieces that will fit without over-crowding and fry, turning the pieces with tongs until they are coloured all over. Remove from the pan using a slotted spoon and set aside. Do this in batches, if necessary.

Add 2 tablespoons oil to any oil remaining in the wok over a medium heat and swirl it around. Add the spice paste and curry powder and stir-fry for 1 minute to cook the out the rawness. Stand back when you add the paste because it will splatter.

Stir in the aubergine, Chinese cabbage, beans, carrots, coconut milk, 250–300ml water and the fried tofu, and bring to the boil. Reduce the heat and leave to simmer, stirring occasionally, for 15 minutes, or until all the vegetables are tender.

Stir in the sugar, squeeze in lime juice to taste and add salt to taste. Adjust the amount of sugar, if necessary and it's ready to serve.

Have you ever gone shopping with a specific shopping list and returned home with completely different ingredients? That is exactly how this rich, spicy curry came into being. I was shopping and I couldn't resist the tiny pea aubergines and shimeji mushrooms – the pea aubergines add a real 'pop' to the texture that balances the silky smoothness of the mushrooms. The coconut gravy has a robust flavour from the mix of red and green chillies and the generous amount of white pepper, and I was pleased with the combination. I serve this with jasmine rice (page 283), and think brown jasmine rice is especially good – the nutty flavour holds up well to the flavour of the coconut gravy.

Coconut Curry with Pea Aubergines, Shimeji Mushrooms & Tempeh
kari terung

150g shimeji mushrooms
  (see Atul's tips, right)
7 tablespoons sunflower oil,
  or as needed
200g tempeh, cut into bite-sized
  pieces
1.5cm piece of galangal, bashed
1.5cm piece of fresh ginger,
  peeled and finely chopped
10 shallots, finely chopped
6–8 fresh or freeze-dried Makrut
  lime leaves, fine central ribs
  removed
3 garlic cloves, chopped
2 lemongrass stalks, outer leaves
  removed and the stalks bashed
  and finely chopped
1 tablespoon ground ginger
1 teaspoon ground turmeric
100g pea aubergines, rinsed
600ml vegetable stock, ideally
  home-made (page 282)

Most likely the shimeji mushrooms will be sold in a punnet with the long stalks attached to a central base. Cut the stalks from the base and discard the base. (Or use it with other vegetables to make vegetable stock, page 282.) Wipe the caps with a damp paper towel, if necessary, then separate into individual stalks. If they are loose, make sure they don't have any grit. Set aside.

Heat a wok over a high heat. Add 1 tablespoon of the oil and swirl it around. Add as many tempeh pieces as will fit without overcrowding, and fry, turning the pieces over with tongs, until lightly coloured. Remove from the pan and continue frying, adding a little more oil, if necessary, until all pieces have been coloured. Set aside.

Reheat the wok over a high heat. Add 5 tablespoons oil and swirl it around. Reduce the heat slightly, add the galangal, ginger, shallots, Makrut lime leaves, garlic and lemongrass with a small pinch of salt, and stir-fry until the shallots become translucent.

400ml coconut milk
1 red onion, halved and sliced
3 fresh red bird's-eye chillies
2 long, thin green chillies, slit
   lengthwise, but left whole
1 teaspoon ground white pepper,
   or to taste
small handful Thai or ordinary
   basil leaves
1 lime, halved
sea salt
chopped coriander leaves,
   to garnish
fried onion rings (see Atul's tip,
   page 101), to garnish

Add the ground ginger and turmeric and continue stir-frying for 30 seconds to cook the spices. Watch closely so nothing burns.

Add the pea aubergines, stir in the stock and bring to the boil. Reduce the heat to very low and leave to simmer for 5 minutes to blend the flavours. Stir in the coconut milk, shimeji mushrooms, red onion, red and green chillies and white pepper. Increase the heat slightly and simmer for about 5 minutes until the pea aubergines are tender.

Stir in the basil leaves and squeeze in lime juice to taste. Taste and adjust the white pepper or salt, if necessary. Garnish with onion rings and serve.

● atul's tips

Shimeji mushrooms are in season in the autumn, but cultivated varieties are available all year round. However, they aren't always easy to find, which is why I grabbed them when I could. That really isn't a problem, though, as other mushroom varieties work just as well in this recipe. Try Asian oysters or shiitakes, or western chestnut, Portobello or even everyday brown-cap mushrooms, all sliced or cut into chunks.

Because this curry has such a pronounced pepper flavour, any hearty winter vegetables make a good substitute for the pea aubergines – small broccoli and cauliflower florets, diced carrots, celeriac or turnips are all suitable options.

Amok is Cambodia's national dish, with the lemongrass, galangal and fresh turmeric providing the distinctive character of this curry. I've kept all those ingredients in the curry paste in this vegan version, for an authentic dining experience. Serve with jasmine rice (page 283).

Aubergine & Broccoli in Coconut Curry
amok

3 tablespoons coconut oil
2 red onions, thinly sliced
4 fresh or dried Makrut lime leaves, fine central ribs removed
2 large aubergines, trimmed and cut into bite-sized pieces
800ml coconut milk
150g broccoli florets and stalks, chopped
200g frozen peas
sea salt
spring onions, sliced, to garnish

For the curry paste
6 garlic cloves, chopped
6 fresh or dried Makrut lime leaves, central ribs removed
2–3 fresh red chillies, ideally Thai chillies, to taste, chopped
15g shallots, chopped
¼ lemongrass stalk, outer layers removed and the stalk bashed and finely chopped
3cm piece of galangal, peeled and finely chopped
1cm piece of fresh turmeric, peeled and grated, or 1 teaspoon ground turmeric
4 tablespoons freshly squeezed lime juice
4 teaspoons grated jaggery or Demerara sugar

First make the curry paste. Put all the ingredients in a food processor and process until a smooth paste forms, scraping down the side of the bowl as necessary. Set aside.

Heat a wok over a high heat. Add the coconut oil and swirl it around until it melts. Add the red onions with a pinch of salt and stir-fry until softened. Add the Makrut lime leaves and aubergine and continue stirring to sear the aubergines.

Lower the heat to medium-high, add the curry paste and stir for 2–3 minutes to cook out the rawness. Stir in the coconut milk and bring to the boil. Reduce the heat to the point where the mixture just simmers and leave for about 10 minutes until the aubergine is half tender.

Stir in the broccoli and a splash of water, if necessary, so there is enough liquid to just cover the vegetables, and simmer for a further 10 minutes. Add the peas and continue simmering until all the vegetables are hot and tender. Taste and adjust the salt, if necessary, then garnish with spring onions and serve.

This traditional curry is said to have originated in ancient times when Muslim traders brought dried spices to what is modern-day Cambodia, resulting in rich and sweet curries like this one – it is intense, with a complex flavour. This is a dish for when you are entertaining and want to serve something special, and like all good curries it can be made in advance and reheated. Serve with jasmine rice (page 283) and sliced baguette.

Saraman Curry
cari saramann

200g green beans, trimmed, halved or quartered
200g new potatoes, scrubbed and quartered
400g tempeh, cut into bite-sized pieces
3 tablespoons Ginger Paste (page 281)
4 tablespoons sunflower oil
800ml coconut milk
5 tablespoons palm or light brown sugar
4 tablespoons vegetarian fish sauce
4 tablespoons tamarind water (see Atul's tip, page 167)
200g skinned unsalted roasted peanuts, plus extra, chopped, to garnish
vegetable stock, ideally home-made (page 282), optional
sea salt

For the Saraman curry paste
3 tablespoons sunflower oil
5cm piece of cinnamon bark
2 teaspoons green cardamom pods
6 garlic cloves, chopped

Put the green beans, new potatoes, tempeh and ginger paste in a large bowl and mix together until the vegetables and tempeh are well coated in the paste. Leave to marinate for 30 minutes.

Meanwhile, make the curry paste. Heat a large wok over a high heat. Add the 3 tablespoons oil and swirl it around. Add all the paste ingredients, except the coriander leaves and stalks and the ground turmeric, and stir-fry for 4–5 minutes until fragrant. Watch closely so nothing catches on the bottom of the pan and burns.

Transfer everything to a food processor. Add the coriander and ground turmeric and process until a smooth paste forms, scraping down the side of the bowl as necessary. Set aside half the paste to use in this recipe, then store the remainder (see Atul's tip, right).

Heat the 4 tablespoons oil in a large saucepan with a lid over a medium heat. Add the coconut milk and bring to the boil, then reduce the heat and simmer, stirring, for 3–4 minutes until the oil and coconut milk combine. Add the green beans, new potatoes, tempeh and reserved curry paste. Cover and leave to simmer for 12–15 minutes, stirring occasionally until the potatoes are almost tender.

3 dried long, thin red chillies,
  stem ends removed
3 shallots, chopped
3 star anise
2–3 blades of mace, to taste
2 lemongrass stalks, outer layers
  removed and the stalks bashed
  and chopped
1 nutmeg, grated
2.5cm piece galangal, peeled
  and chopped
100g coriander leaves and stalks,
  chopped
½ teaspoon ground turmeric
vegetable stock (page 282),
  ideally home-made, optional

Stir in the sugar, fish sauce, tamarind water and peanuts with salt to taste. Re-cover the pan and simmer over a very low heat for 2 minutes, or until the potatoes are tender. If the sauce is a bit too thick, stir in the vegetable stock to reach the correct consistency and stir until hot. Taste and adjust the seasoning with salt or fish sauce, if necessary. Sprinkle with chopped peanuts and serve.

● atul's tip

It's difficult to make the Saraman paste in a smaller quantity, so I suggest you freeze half. It freezes well, and if you have coconut milk and peanuts in the cupboard, you've got the basics of a quickly made curry on standby, perfect for lazy weekends or after a busy work day. Store in a covered container in the fridge for up to 1 week, or freeze for up to 3 months.

Typical of many vegetable curries from Cambodia, this recipe contains sweet potatoes, and I've added taro for variety. If you can't find taro, substitute a floury potato, such as King Edward, or just make up the difference with extra sweet potatoes.

Khmer Vegetable Curry
cari banle khmer

2 tablespoons sunflower oil
300g sweet potatoes, peeled and cut into bite-sized pieces
300g taro, peeled and cut into bite-sized pieces
800ml coconut milk
6 fresh or freeze-dried Makrut lime leaves, central ribs removed
2 carrots, peeled and cut into 0.5cm slices
4 tablespoon vegetarian fish sauce, or to taste
1 tablespoon palm sugar
100g green beans, trimmed and chopped
100g frozen peas
handful of bean sprouts, to garnish

For the curry paste
6–8 dried long, thin red chillies, to taste, soaked in hot water
2.5cm piece of cinnamon bark
4 star anise
1 teaspoon coriander seeds
4 tablespoons Cambodian Spice Paste (page 277)
4 tablespoons chopped coriander stems and roots
2 tablespoons freshly grated orange zest
1 teaspoon vegetarian fish sauce

First, make the curry paste. When the chillies are rehydrated, drain, remove the stem ends, deseed and set aside. Heat a dry wok over a medium heat. Add the cinnamon bark, star anise and coriander seeds, and stir-fry until aromatic. Tip the spices on to a plate and leave to cool.

When the spices are cool, transfer them to a food processor. Add the chillies and the remaining curry paste ingredients and process until a paste forms, scraping down the side of the bowl as necessary.

Reheat the wok over a high heat. Add the oil and swirl it around. Add the curry paste and stir-fry until it turns light brown. Reduce the heat slightly, add the sweet potatoes and taro and stir until they are coated in the paste. Add the coconut milk, Makrut lime leaves, carrots, fish sauce, sugar and 100ml water, stirring to dissolve the sugar. Bring to the boil, then reduce the heat and leave to simmer for 15 minutes, stirring occasionally, until the vegetables are almost tender.

Add the green beans and continue simmering for 4 minutes. Stir in the peas and continue simmering for a further 1–2 minutes until the peas are hot and all the vegetables are tender. Taste and adjust the amount of fish sauce, if necessary, garnish with the bean sprouts then serve.

I was fortunate enough to grow up eating many mango curries, but this mango curry is very special to me – the recipe was given to me by a young Cambodian chef who worked for me at Tamarind, in London's Mayfair, when I was awarded my first Michelin star. It's the curry paste that elevates this dish to a higher level, with richness from the candlenuts.

Mango & Tempeh Curry
cari svay

1 tablespoon sunflower oil
2 mangoes, halved, stoned and
   flesh cut away in cubes
200ml water
2 tablespoons palm or light
   brown sugar
500g tempeh or seitan, cut into
   bite-sized cubes
400ml coconut milk
8 baby tomatoes, quartered
sea salt
spring onions, chopped,
   to garnish

For the curry paste
4–6 candlenuts or
   macadamia nuts
2 fresh red bird's-eye chillies,
   coarsely chopped
3 shallots, chopped
2 thick lemongrass stalks, outer
   leaves removed and the stalks
   bashed and chopped
1 long, thin green chilli,
   coarsely chopped

First, make the curry paste. Put all the paste ingredients in a food processor and process until a fine paste forms, scraping down the side of the bowl as necessary. Alternatively, you can use a pestle and mortar.

Heat a large wok over a high heat. Add the oil and swirl it around. Reduce the heat slightly, add the curry paste and stir-fry until it is lightly coloured. It's important to cook the shallots at this point, and don't stop stirring, because the paste can quickly burn.

Add the mangoes and stir until all the pieces are coated in the paste. Stir in the water, sugar and a pinch of salt. Bring to the boil, then reduce the heat and simmer just until the mangoes begin to soften.

Add the tempeh, coconut milk and tomatoes, and bring to the boil. Reduce the heat and simmer for a further 5–7 minutes until the tomatoes begin to break down and the flavours blend. Taste and adjust the salt, if necessary. Garnish with spring onions and serve.

This is a simple, straightforward one-pot wonder. I particularly like Vietnamese food, as I think it is interesting how cooks combine the use of spices as Indians do, but with Chinese cooking methods. I would not automatically have thought to put aubergine and mushrooms together in a recipe, but it was something I tried while developing this recipe and I think the combination works very well. Like many curries, this is good made in advance and reheated. It's best to add the cashew nuts just before serving. If you do add them in advance and leave them in the curry before reheating, they will soften a little, but still provide a pleasant crunch. Serve this with jasmine rice (page 283).

Vegan Curry
thuan chay kari

150g cassava, peeled and cut into bite-sized chunks (see Atul's tip, right)
2 tablespoons sunflower oil
1.5cm piece of fresh ginger, peeled and chopped
3 garlic cloves, chopped
1 banana shallot, chopped
1 teaspoon chopped lemongrass
1 tablespoon chilli paste
200g firm tofu, patted dry, cut into bite-sized pieces
1 aubergine, trimmed and cut into bite-sized pieces
1 carrot, peeled and thinly sliced
2 teaspoons Chinese five-spice powder
½ teaspoon ground coriander
¼ teaspoon red chilli powder
100g broccoli florets, halved
100g brown-cap mushrooms, trimmed and sliced
400ml coconut milk
250ml water

Put the cassava chunks in a large saucepan of salted water and bring to the boil. Cover the pan and boil for 25 minutes or until tender.

Meanwhile, heat a wok over a high heat. Add the oil and swirl around. Reduce the heat to medium-high, add the ginger, garlic, shallot and lemongrass, and stir-fry for 1 minute to cook out the rawness. Reduce the heat to low, add the chilli paste and continue stirring for 30 seconds or so.

Add the tofu, aubergine and carrot, and continue stir-frying so they are well coated and start to absorb the flavours. Stir in the five-spice powder, ground coriander and chilli powder, and stir for 30 seconds to cook the ground spices.

Stir in the broccoli and mushrooms, then add the coconut milk, water, brown sugar and salt to taste. Bring to the boil, then reduce the heat and leave to simmer for about 20 minutes until all the vegetables are tender.

1 teaspoon soft light brown
  sugar, or to taste
1½ tablespoons freshly squeezed
  lime juice, or to taste
8–10 unsalted cashew nuts,
  lightly toasted
sea salt
chopped spring onions,
  to garnish

When the cassava is tender, use a slotted spoon
to transfer it to the curry. Add the lime juice, taste
and adjust the sugar and salt, if necessary. Stir in
the cashew nuts for a little crunch, garnish with
chopped spring onion and serve.

atul's tip

Cassava is a starchy root vegetable eaten throughout
Southeast Asia, providing variety from potatoes. It
takes longer to cook than the other vegetables in
this recipe, however, which is why I say to parboil
it first. Once the cassava and other vegetables are
combined, you can turn off the heat and leave the
curry for reheating later or the following day -- the
cassava will continue to absorb flavours. If you don't
want to use cassava, try taro or ordinary potatoes.

This straightforward curry is a perfect meal when you are short on time, and it will taste great reheated the following day. The heat comes from the paprika and is a subtle, background flavour. I've included a small handful of mangetout, and I don't think you should omit them as they add crunch and a good splash of colour. Serve with plenty of jasmine rice (page 283) to soak up the delicious gravy.

Jackfruit & Tofu Curry

qua mit va dau hu cari

2 tablespoons sunflower oil
200g spring onions, finely chopped, with some set aside to garnish
5 garlic cloves, finely chopped
3cm piece of fresh ginger, peeled and finely chopped
1 tablespoon ground coriander
1 teaspoon ground cinnamon
1 teaspoon ground cumin
1 teaspoon hot paprika
1 teaspoon coarsely ground black peppercorns
1 teaspoon ground turmeric
2 x 400g cans jackfruit pieces, drained
400ml coconut milk
300ml vegetable stock, ideally home-made (page 282), plus a little extra, if needed
2 tablespoons vegetarian fish sauce, or to taste
400g firm tofu, cut into bite-sized pieces
200g sweet potatoes, peeled and cut into bite-sized pieces
100g mangetout, trimmed
lime wedges, to serve

Heat a wok over a high heat. Add the oil and swirl it around. Add the spring onions, garlic and ginger, and stir-fry until they are fragrant. Add the ground coriander, cinnamon, cumin, paprika, ground black peppercorns and turmeric, and continue stir-frying for 30 seconds to cook the ground spices. Watch closely so nothing burns.

Reduce the heat, add the jackfruit pieces and stir until they are well coated in spices. Add the coconut milk, vegetable stock and fish sauce, then stir in the tofu and sweet potatoes. Bring to the boil, stirring, then reduce the heat and leave to simmer for 15 minutes.

Add the mangetout to the wok and continue simmering for a further 5–10 minutes until the potatoes and mangetout are tender but the mangetout still have a little crunch. If the sauce looks like it's evaporating too much, stir in extra vegetable stock or water. Garnish with spring onions and serve with lime wedges for squeezing over at the table.

I love the way the broccoli retains its crispness in this uncomplicated recipe, with its combination of spiciness and saltiness. For variety, replace the broccoli with thinly sliced bok choy. Serve this with plenty of steamed jasmine rice (page 283).

Broccoli & Garlic Stir-fry
xao bong cai xanh va toi

2 tablespoons sesame oil

2.5cm piece of lemongrass stalks, outer layers removed and the stalk bashed and finely chopped

4 garlic cloves, chopped

1 fresh red chilli, finely chopped

¼ teaspoon red chilli flakes

500g tenderstem broccoli florets and stalks, trimmed

½ red onion, or 1 shallot, finely chopped

vegetarian fish sauce

soy sauce

3 spring onions, trimmed and finely chopped

1 teaspoon grated jaggery or Demerara sugar

chilli oil, to garnish

Heat a large wok with a lid over a high heat. Add the sesame oil and swirl it around. Add the lemongrass, garlic, red chilli and chilli flakes, and stir-fry to flavour the oil.

Add the broccoli and red onion and continue stir-frying so they are well coated with the spices. Add vegetarian fish sauce to taste with a generous drizzle of soy sauce and continue stir-frying until the broccoli starts to become tender.

Stir in the spring onions and jaggery, add a splash of water, cover the wok and leave the broccoli to steam for 1 minute or until tender. Taste and adjust the fish sauce and soy sauce, if necessary. Drizzle over chilli oil to garnish and serve.

Left: Broccoli & Garlic
Stir-fry (page 47)
Right: Pineapple & Tempeh
Skewers (page 50)

Grilled pineapple gives a fresh, sweet flavour to these easy-to-prepare skewers. The dipping sauce can be made up to a day in advance and chilled until required, and the skewers can be marinated and assembled in advance, ready for last-minute grilling. I like to serve this with a fresh salad of shredded Chinese cabbage, sliced cucumber and bean sprouts, tossed with coriander, mint and Thai basil leaves with a sprinkling of sea salt and fresh lime juice squeezed over.

Pineapple & Tempeh Skewers
tvai dua va tempeh xien que

½ fresh pineapple, peeled, cored and cut into 2.5cm pieces
400g tempeh, cut into 2.5cm pieces
sunflower oil for basting
2 spring onions, sliced on the diagonal, to garnish, optional
black and white sesame seeds, to garnish, optional

For the marinade
6 garlic cloves, finely chopped
2 long, thin green chillies, finely chopped
1 lemongrass stalk, outer layers removed and the stalk bashed and finely chopped
1 tablespoon vegetarian fish sauce
1 tablespoon dark soy sauce or tamari
1 tablespoon sunflower oil
2 teaspoons rice wine vinegar
1 teaspoon palm or light brown sugar

If using bamboo or wooden skewers put 12 skewers in a bowl of water and leave to soak for 1 hour.

Meanwhile, mix all the marinade ingredients together in a large bowl, stirring to dissolve the sugar. Add the pineapple and tempeh and gently stir so the pieces are well coated. Set aside and leave to marinate for at least 1 hour, or cover and chill for up to 6 hours.

To make the dipping sauce, dissolve the sugar in the boiling water in a non-metallic bowl. Pound the garlic with the chilli to make a paste, then mix with the sugar water. Stir in the vegetarian fish sauce, vinegar and lime juice. Set aside until required.

When you are ready to cook, light a charcoal barbecue and leave until the coals are glowing, or preheat a grill to high and line a grill pan with aluminium foil.

Gently thread the pineapple and tempeh pieces alternately on the soaked skewers. Brush the barbecue grid or grill rack with oil, then add the skewers and grill, basting with the marinade and turning so they colour evenly. You want a nice golden colour on the pineapple and tempeh.

For the *nuoc cham* (dipping sauce)

2 teaspoons palm or light brown sugar

100ml water, boiling

2 garlic cloves, peeled and crushed

1 fresh red chilli, very finely chopped

2 tablespoons vegetarian fish sauce

1 tablespoon rice wine vinegar

freshly squeezed juice of 1 lime

Transfer the skewers to a platter and sprinkle with spring onions and sesame seeds. Serve hot with the dipping sauce on the side.

● **atul's tips**

Lemongrass gives its distinctive flavour to curries and other simmered or braised dishes throughout all of east Asia, especially Vietnam, Malaysia and Thailand. Cut off the base, then remove the dried outer leaves. Bash the remaining stalk to help release the wonderful fresh flavour. The stalks can be left whole, or chopped or puréed if they are an integral part of a sauce or paste.

You can buy jars of chopped lemongrass but nothing beats using the fresh stalks. Buy a bunch and freeze what you aren't immediately using for up to 6 months.

Here's my version of Laos' national dish – a warm salad with crunch from toasted rice grains. I first encountered *larb* when I saw a traditional beef version being demonstrated by food writer Tom Parker Bowles, and I decided almost instantly I wanted to capture all the fresh flavours in a vegetarian recipe. I've used two widely available types of Asian mushroom here, but big, chunky Portobello mushrooms would also be good.

Warm Mixed Mushroom Salad
het larb

1 tablespoon white or brown basmati rice
3 tablespoons sunflower oil
2 red onions, finely chopped
300g oyster mushrooms, trimmed and finely chopped
300g shiitake mushrooms, trimmed and coarsely chopped
5cm piece of lemongrass, outer layers removed and the stalk bashed and finely chopped
2 garlic cloves, finely chopped
1 fresh red bird's-eye chilli, chopped, plus extra to garnish
1 teaspoon vegetarian fish sauce
Baby Gem lettuce, the leaves separated into 8 'cups'
sliced spring onion, to garnish

For the dressing
1 teaspoon vegetarian fish sauce
1 teaspoon grated jaggery or Demerara sugar
freshly squeezed juice of 2 limes
2 teaspoons red chilli paste
2.5cm piece of lemongrass, outer layers removed and the stalk finely chopped

Heat a dry wok over a medium-high heat. Add the rice and toast, stirring constantly, until it is golden brown. Immediately tip the rice out of the pan and set aside.

To make the dressing, stir the fish sauce, jaggery and lime juice together in a non-metallic bowl until the jaggery dissolves. Add the chilli paste and stir until blended, then stir in the lemongrass. Set aside.

When you are ready to cook the main ingredients, reheat the wok over a high heat. Add the oil and swirl it around. Reduce the heat slightly, add the red onion and stir-fry until softened. Add the oyster and shiitake mushrooms, the lemongrass, garlic, red chilli and fish sauce, and stir-fry until the mushrooms are tender.

Turn off the heat and stir in the dressing, reserving 1 tablespoon. Divide the mushroom mixture among the lettuce cups. Drizzle over the reserved dressing, garnish with the toasted rice, sliced red chillies and spring onions and serve.

I like the way the sweetness of the pineapple and the relative blandness of the tofu balance the heat of the curry paste in this simple dish – it's sweet and hot with subtle flavours from the herbs. Unlike in neighbouring Asian countries, where jasmine rice is the ubiquitous accompaniment to most curries, Laotians favour sticky rice (page 284). Fragrant curries like this are typically served with fresh greens alongside, so I recommend the Broccoli & Garlic Stir-fry (page 47) or one of the many varieties of Chinese cabbage. When fresh bamboo shoots are available, don't hesitate to try them.

Pineapple & Tofu Curry
apple ak nad lae tao hu aekng

2 tablespoons sunflower oil
4 fresh Makrut or freeze-dried Makrut lime leaves, fine central ribs removed
2 tablespoons vegetarian fish sauce, or to taste
1 tablespoon palm or light brown sugar
400ml coconut milk
400g firm tofu, cut into bite-sized pieces
½ pineapple, peeled, cored and cut into bite-sized pieces
100g mangetout, trimmed
4 spring onions, chopped
sea salt
Thai basil or ordinary basil leaves, shredded, to garnish

For the Laotian curry paste
1 teaspoon coriander seeds
½ teaspoon cumin seeds
2 fresh red Thai or bird's-eye chillies, chopped
1.5cm piece of fresh galangal, peeled and finely chopped

First, make the curry paste. Heat a dry wok over a medium heat. Add the coriander and cumin seeds and stir-fry until the seeds start to darken and pop, then immediately tip them on to a plate.

When the seeds are cool, transfer them to a spice grinder or coffee grinder with the remaining paste ingredients and process until a smooth paste forms, scraping down the side of the bowl, as necessary. Alternatively, pound all the ingredients in a pestle and mortar. Set aside half the paste to use in this recipe, then store the remainder (see Atul's tip, right).

Reheat the wok over a high heat. Add the oil and swirl it around. Reduce the heat slightly, then add the reserved curry paste and stir-fry for until it is fragrant. Add the Makrut lime leaves, fish sauce and sugar, and continue stir-frying until the sugar dissolves. Watch closely so the paste doesn't catch on the bottom of the pan and burn.

Stir in the coconut milk and bring to the boil, stirring. Add the tofu, pineapple and mangetout, reduce the heat and leave to simmer until the mangetout are tender, but still with a little crunch. Stir in the spring onions and continue simmering

1.5cm piece of fresh ginger, peeled and chopped
1.5cm piece of fresh turmeric, peeled and chopped, or 1 teaspoon ground turmeric
2 garlic cloves, peeled
½ lemongrass stalk, outer layers removed and the stalk bashed and finely chopped
½ shallot, chopped
1½ tablespoons finely chopped coriander roots
2 tablespoons water
1 tablespoon sunflower oil
1½ teaspoons medium curry powder of your choice
1 teaspoon vegetarian fish sauce
½ teaspoon ground turmeric
finely grated zest and juice of ½ Makrut or ordinary lime

for another minute or so to blend the flavours. Adjust the seasoning with fish sauce and add salt if necessary. Garnish with shredded basil leaves and serve.

● **atul's tip**

It's not practical to make this curry paste in a smaller quantity – and once the paste has been made this is a very quick curry to prepare – so it's worth having an extra portion on hand. The leftover paste can be stored in a covered container in the fridge for up to 1 week, or frozen for up to 3 months.

I doubt many Japanese cooks would start making the katsu curry sauce by frying the red chilli and shallot, but I wanted to intensify the flavours. This curry is more time-consuming than most recipes in this book, but you can make both the curry powder and katsu curry sauce in advance. Serve this with plain sticky rice (page 284) and a selection of Japanese pickled vegetables, such as cucumbers and carrots, and/or sushi ginger. Peeled sweet potatoes are a good alternative for the aubergine.

Aubergine & Tofu Katsu Curry
nasu to tofukatsu karei

75g panko breadcrumbs
½ teaspoon cayenne pepper or red chilli powder, or to taste
¼ teaspoon black and/or white sesame seeds, optional
⅛ teaspoon ground turmeric
2 tablespoons rice flour mixed with 4 tablespoons water to make a thin paste
200g firm tofu, pressed (see Atul's tip, page 75), patted dry and cut into 5cm sticks, about 1cm thick
1 large aubergine, cut into about 1cm thick slices
sunflower oil, for deep-frying
sea salt
fresh red chillies, thinly sliced on the diagonal, to garnish
spring onions, thinly sliced on the diagonal, to garnish

For the Japanese curry powder
1 dried bay leaf
1 star anise
¾ teaspoon fennel seeds
⅛ teaspoon fenugreek seeds
⅛ teaspoon dried sage

First make the curry powder. Put the bay leaf, star anise, fennel seeds, fenugreek seeds and sage in a spice grinder or coffee grinder and grind until a powder forms. Pass through a fine sieve into a bowl then add all the ground spices and mix together. Set aside 2 teaspoons to use in the sauce and store the remainder in an airtight container in a dark place for up to 6 months.

To make the curry sauce, heat the oil in a large saucepan over a medium-high heat. Add the red chilli and shallot and fry, stirring, for 30 seconds or so to flavour the oil. Reduce the heat to medium and stir the tomato purée into the oil. Add the 2 teaspoons curry powder and the garlic powder, and continue stirring for 30 seconds to cook the spices.

Stir in the vegetable stock and coconut milk with a pinch of salt. Add the rice flour paste and slowly bring to the boil, stirring constantly, until the sauce thickens and coats the back of the spoon. Remove from the heat and set aside.

When you are ready to cook, preheat the oven to 150°C/Fan 130°C/Gas 2 and line a baking tray with kitchen paper. Put the breadcrumbs in a shallow bowl, add the cayenne pepper, sesame

1 tablespoon ground turmeric

1½ teaspoons ground coriander

1½ teaspoons ground cumin

1½ teaspoons ground
  black pepper

¾ teaspoon red chilli powder

scant ½ teaspoon ground
  cardamom

¼ teaspoon ground allspice

¼ teaspoon ground cloves

⅛ teaspoon ground cinnamon

a pinch of ground nutmeg

For the katsu curry sauce

1 tablespoon sunflower oil

1 fresh red bird's-eye chilli,
  finely chopped

1 shallot, chopped

1 tablespoon tomato purée

2 teaspoons Japanese Curry
  Powder (see above)

½ teaspoon garlic powder

500ml vegetable stock, ideally
  home-made (page 282)

200ml coconut milk

4 tablespoons rice flour
  or cornflour mixed with
  6 tablespoons water to
  make a thin paste

seeds, if using, turmeric and a pinch of salt, and mix together. Put the rice flour paste in another shallow bowl. Using a pair of tongs, take one piece of tofu or aubergine at a time and run it through the flour paste until lightly coated, then toss it in the breadcrumbs until coated. Set aside and continue until all the aubergine and tofu pieces are coated.

Heat enough oil for deep-frying in a deep-fat fryer or a heavy-based saucepan until it reaches 180°C. Add as many tofu pieces as will fit without over-crowding and deep-fry, moving them around with tongs or a slotted spoon, until golden brown. Using a slotted spoon, remove from the oil, transfer to the lined baking tray and keep hot in the oven. Repeat with the remaining tofu and aubergine pieces until they are all fried, reheating the oil between batches, if necessary.

Just before serving, reheat the katsu curry sauce. Divide the crisp tofu and aubergine pieces among 4 plates and add a portion of sauce. Garnish with red chillies and spring onions and serve.

● atul's tip

The panko-coated tofu and aubergine can also be oven-baked, rather than fried. Preheat the oven to 220°C/Fan 200°C/Gas 7. Coat the tofu and aubergine pieces as above and place on a baking sheet lined with baking paper. Drizzle generously with olive or sunflower oil and bake in the oven for 15–20 minutes until soft and starting to brown. Increase the temperature to 240°C/Fan 220°C/Gas 8 and bake for a further 10 minutes for the crumbs to crisp. Reheat the curry sauce and serve as above.

Known as 'chettiar curry', this recipe hails from the 19th century. When the British took control of Burma in 1826, a large Indian population migrated to Burma, especially from south India, taking their culinary traditions with them. Many of the immigrants became landlords known as *chettiars*, and this dish would be served to their labourers. It's not unusual for this to be served at room temperature, but always with hot sticky rice (page 284).

Burmese Vegetable Curry
hintheesone kala hin

100g split yellow peas (*toor daal* or pigeon peas), rinsed and soaked in cold water to cover for 20 minutes

2 tablespoons sunflower oil

1 teaspoon cumin seeds

1 onion, thinly sliced

1 dried bay leaf

1 tablespoon ground coriander

1 teaspoon red chilli powder

1 teaspoon ground cumin

½ teaspoon ground turmeric

1 tablespoon tamarind water (see Atul's tip, page 167)

200g yellow or orange pumpkin or butternut squash, peeled, deseeded and cut into bite-sized cubes

2 small, thin aubergines, cut into 0.5cm slices

2 carrots, peeled and chopped

2 floury potatoes, such as King Edwards, peeled and cut into bite-sized pieces

1 small mooli, peeled and cut into 0.5cm slices

1 litre vegetable stock, ideally home-made (page 282)

sea salt

chopped coriander, to garnish

First, prepare the split yellow peas. Drain and then put them in a saucepan over a high heat with plenty of water to cover and a pinch of salt. Bring to the boil, skimming the surface as necessary, and simmer for 20 minutes or until just tender. Drain well and set aside.

Heat a large dry wok over a high heat. Add the oil and swirl it around. Reduce the heat to medium, add the cumin seeds and stir-fry until they crackle. Add the onion and continue stir-frying until the onion is translucent. Stir in the bay leaf, ground coriander, chilli powder, cumin, turmeric and the split yellow peas, and continue stirring for 30 seconds to cook the ground spices. Watch closely so they don't burn.

Stir in the tamarind water with the pumpkin, aubergines, carrots, potatoes and mooli, and stir until the vegetables are well coated in the spices.

Pour in the stock and bring to the boil. Reduce the heat and leave the vegetables and split yellow peas to simmer for 10–12 minutes until they are all tender. You should be able to squeeze the split peas between your fingers. Taste and adjust the salt, if necessary. Garnish with coriander leaves and serve.

I find that most Asians adore cooking with and eating aubergines, and the Burmese are no exception. Aubergines have a neutral flavour on their own, so it's not really surprising they are so popular – once you combine them with all the other aromatic and spicy ingredients available to Asian cooks, aubergines act like a sponge and come alive. Stir-fried choi sum or spinach is good with this, and even cooked green lentils would work.

Aubergine & Sweet Potato Curry

hkaramsee nhang kaanhcwannu hainn

1 tablespoon vegetarian
  fish sauce
1 teaspoon ground turmeric
400g aubergine, trimmed and
  cut into bite-sized pieces
2 onions, peeled and finely
  chopped
3 large dried red chillies, soaked
  in hot water to cover for at
  least 20 minutes
2 tablespoons sunflower or
  rapeseed oil
4 garlic cloves, finely chopped
2 sweet potatoes, peeled and
  cut into bite-sized pieces
100g green beans, topped and
  tailed, and halved or quartered
600ml vegetable stock, ideally
  home-made (page 282)
1 teaspoon sweet paprika
sea salt
chopped coriander leaves,
  to garnish

Mix the fish sauce, turmeric and a pinch of salt together in a bowl. Add the aubergine, mix well together and leave to marinate for 20 minutes.

Meanwhile, put the onions in a food processor and process on and off until a rough paste forms, scraping down the side of the bowl as necessary. Set aside.

When the chillies are rehydrated, drain them well and remove the stem ends. Set aside.

Heat a wok with a lid over a high heat. Add the oil and swirl it around. Reduce the heat slightly, add the garlic, onion paste and chillies, and stir-fry until the onion paste is caramelised. It's important to cook the rawness out of the onions at this point, but watch closely because they can burn quickly. If you think the mixture is starting to catch on the base of the wok, stir in a little water.

Stir in the aubergine with any remaining marinade, the sweet potatoes, green beans, vegetable stock, paprika and a pinch of salt, but remember the aubergine has been salted. Bring to the boil, then reduce the heat to low, cover the wok and leave the vegetables to simmer for 10–12 minutes until they are all tender. Taste and adjust the salt, if necessary. Garnish with the coriander and it's ready to serve.

Serves 4

Thai green curries are a favourite of mine, and I like them spicy hot with a hint of sweetness, which is what you get with this recipe. The green curry paste I suggest using in this recipe (page 278) is my version of one shared with me many years ago from my good friend, chef David Thompson. He's the go-to expert on Thai cuisine, so you just know this is going to be good.

Thai Green Curry
kaeng khiao gan

2 tablespoons coconut oil
250g Green Thai Curry Paste
  (page 278)
200g brown-cap mushrooms,
  trimmed and quartered
150g aubergine, trimmed and
  cut into bite-sized pieces
5 baby corn cobs, trimmed and
  halved on the diagonal
1 red onion, chopped
400ml coconut milk
1 tablespoon freshly squeezed
  lime juice, or to taste
1 tablespoon soy sauce,
  or to taste
1 teaspoon soft light brown
  sugar, or to taste
100g mangetout or sugar-snap
  peas
75g baby spinach leaves, rinsed
100g coriander leaves, finely
  chopped
2 tablespoons chopped Thai
  or ordinary basil leaves

Heat a large wok with a lid over a high heat. Add the coconut oil and swirl it around until it melts. Add the curry paste and stir-fry for 1 minute to cook out the rawness. Add the mushrooms, aubergine, baby corn cobs and red onion, and continue stir-frying until the onion is translucent.

Add the coconut milk and bring to the boil, stirring. Add the lime juice, soy sauce and sugar, and leave to simmer, covered, for 12–15 minutes until the aubergine is almost tender.

Stir in the mangetout, spinach and the coriander and basil leaves, and add a little water to just cover the vegetables, if necessary. Leave to simmer, uncovered, for a further 5–7 minutes until the mangetout are tender. Taste and adjust the lime juice, soy sauce and sugar, if necessary. It's ready to serve.

No one single Thai meal influenced this fragrant, spicy curry. Instead, on a cold winter's day in London when I was developing recipes, I let my memory transport me back to my culinary adventure in Phuket Town, savouring the aromas and flavours of the many curries I enjoyed. Jasmine rice (page 283) is the obvious accompaniment, and I'd put this in the middle of the table with other dishes and let everyone help themselves.

Red Vegetable Curry, Phuket Style
kaeng phet

3 tablespoons coconut oil

1 onion, halved and thinly sliced

2cm piece of fresh ginger, peeled and finely chopped

8 new potatoes, scrubbed and cut into bite-sized chunks

4 garlic cloves, finely chopped

1 red pepper, cored, deseeded and thinly sliced

1 small head cauliflower, cut into florets

250g Thai Red Curry Paste (page 279)

800ml coconut milk

500ml vegetable stock, ideally home-made (page 282)

150g carrots, peeled and cut into julienned strips or coarsely grated

1 courgette, halved lengthwise and sliced

1 tablespoon vegetarian fish sauce

1 tablespoon freshly squeezed lime juice, or to taste

100g baby spinach leaves, rinsed and shaken dry

15 Thai basil or ordinary basil leaves

Heat a large wok over a high heat. Add the coconut oil and swirl it around until it melts. Add the onion and stir-fry until it's translucent. Add the ginger, potatoes, garlic and red pepper, and continue stir-frying until the onion becomes light brown. This is an important step because you are also cooking the rawness out of the garlic and ginger, but don't take your eyes off the wok, because everything can quickly catch and burn.

Add the cauliflower florets and curry paste and keep stirring so all the ingredients are well coated, then stir-fry for a further minute to cook the paste. Stir in the coconut milk and stock and bring to the boil. Reduce the heat and leave to simmer for 12–15 minutes, stirring occasionally, until the cauliflower and potatoes are just tender.

Add the carrots and courgette and continue simmering for 3–4 minutes until they are both tender. Season with the vegetarian fish sauce and lime juice, then stir in the spinach and tear in the basil. When the spinach wilts, the curry is ready to serve.

Serves 4

I don't think anyone will deny that tofu on its own can be boring. It needs a partner. I often partner it with lentils, but for this recipe I experimented with chickpeas, and I'm pleased with the result. This goes well with jasmine rice (page 283) or rice noodles. I also recommend brown jasmine rice here, which is available online if you have difficulty finding it.

Tofu & Chickpea Curry
kaeng teahu laea thaw chik phi

2 tablespoons coconut oil
1cm piece fresh ginger, peeled and finely chopped
2 garlic cloves, finely chopped
1 teaspoon finely chopped fresh red chilli, ideally a Thai chilli, or to taste
½ lemongrass stalk, outer layers removed and the stalk bashed
½ red onion, halved and thinly sliced
1 small red pepper, cored, deseeded and finely chopped
1 teaspoon ground coriander
½ teaspoon cayenne pepper
½ teaspoon sweet paprika
250g small broccoli florets
1 can (400g) chickpeas, drained and rinsed
400g firm tofu, cut into bite-sized cubes
1 tablespoon tamari or soy sauce
800ml coconut milk
100g mangetout, chopped
2 handfuls baby spinach leaves, rinsed and shaken dry
a handful Thai basil or ordinary basil leaves

Heat a wok over a high heat. Add the coconut milk and swirl around until it melts. Add the ginger, garlic and red chilli, and stir-fry stir for 1 minute to cook out the rawness from the garlic and ginger and to flavour the oil. Add the lemongrass and red onion and continue stir-frying until the onion is translucent. Watch closely so nothing catches and burns.

Stir in the red pepper, then stir in the ground coriander, cayenne and paprika, and continue stir-frying for 30 seconds to cook the ground spices. Add the broccoli florets, chickpeas and tofu, and continue stirring, being careful not to break up the tofu.

Add the tamari and stir to flavour the tofu. Pour in the coconut milk and bring to the boil. Reduce the heat and leave to simmer for 5–8 minutes until the broccoli is almost tender.

Add the mangetout, spinach leaves and basil leaves. Return the curry to the boil, then reduce the heat and simmer until the mangetout is just cooked, but still with some crunch. Taste and adjust the amount of tamari, if necessary. It's ready to serve.

Serves 4

Pad Thai must be one of the most universally popular Thai dishes. This vegan version takes me straight back to Bangkok's food stalls – the vibrancy of the hawkers' stalls is as exciting as the delicious flavours. My teenage son told me off for not making more when I was recipe testing! I hope you enjoy this dish as much as he does.

Pad Thai

3 tablespoons sunflower oil

2 carrots, peeled and cut with a spiralizer or grated lengthways

2 courgettes, trimmed and cut with a spiralizer or grated lengthways

2 red peppers, cored, deseeded and thinly sliced

1 onion, halved and thinly sliced

1cm piece of galangal, peeled and finely chopped, or use extra fresh ginger

¼ lemongrass stalk, outer layers removed and the stalk bashed and finely chopped

200g dried medium rice noodles, soaked in hot water to cover for 20 minutes

2cm piece of fresh ginger, peeled and finely chopped

For the pad Thai sauce

2 tablespoons vegetarian fish sauce

2 tablespoons soft brown sugar

2 teaspoons soy sauce

1 teaspoon chilli purée or sauce

To garnish (optional)

3 tablespoons unsalted peanuts, lightly toasted and crushed

finely shredded basil leaves

finely chopped coriander leaves

First, make the pad Thai sauce by mixing all the ingredients together with 2 tablespoons water. Set aside.

Heat 2 tablespoons of oil in a large wok over a high heat. Swirl it around the wok to coat the base. Add the carrots, courgettes, red peppers, onion, galangal and half the lemongrass, and stir-fry until the vegetables are tender. Tip the vegetables out of the wok and set aside.

Drain the noodles, shaking off as much water as possible. Wipe out the wok, then reheat over a medium-high heat. Add the remaining 1 tablespoon oil and swirl around. Add the remaining lemongrass and the ginger and stir-fry for 1 minute to cook out the rawness. Add the noodles to the wok with the pad Thai sauce. Return the vegetables to the wok and stir-fry until the noodles are tender and hot and all the ingredients are well combined.

Remove from the wok, using a spoon and fork to separate the noodles. Garnish with chopped peanuts, basil and coriander, if using, and serve.

I first ate this at a friend's home in Bangkok, and I loved the perfect balance of sweet and spicy, with the lime juice added at the end to cut through the richness. My friend's cook didn't speak English and I don't speak Thai, so my friend translated as I scribbled down the details. Serve with brown jasmine rice (page 283) or rice noodles.

Yellow Mango & Coconut Curry
kaeng heluxng mamwng

75g unsalted cashew nuts

2 tablespoons sunflower oil, rapeseed oil or coconut oil

2cm piece of fresh ginger, peeled and finely chopped

2 garlic cloves, finely chopped

1 fresh red bird's-eye chilli, finely chopped

2 tablespoons finely chopped shallot

1 red pepper, cored, deseeded and chopped

3 tablespoons Thai Red Curry Paste (page 279)

1 teaspoon ground turmeric

150g cored red cabbage, finely chopped

2 tablespoons grated jaggery or Demerara sugar

2 teaspoons tamari or soy sauce

400ml coconut milk

2 ripe mangoes, stoned, flesh cut into bite-sized chunks and removed from the peel

75g frozen peas

3 tablespoons freshly squeezed lime juice, or to taste

2 tablespoons chopped coriander leaves

Thai basil or ordinary basil leaves, to garnish, optional

Heat a large dry wok over a medium-high heat. Add the cashew nuts and toast, stirring, until lightly browned. Tip out of the pan and set aside.

Re-heat the wok. Add the oil and swirl it around. Add the ginger and garlic and stir-fry for 1 minute to cook the spices and flavour the oil. Add the red chilli and shallot and continue stir-frying until the shallot softens.

Add the red pepper, red curry paste and turmeric, and stir-fry. Add the red cabbage, jaggery and tamari sauce, and continue stir-frying until the jaggery dissolves. Stir in the coconut milk and bring to the boil. Reduce the heat and simmer, stirring occasionally, for about 5 minutes until the pepper is almost tender.

Add the mangoes, peas and toasted cashew nuts to the wok, then stir in the lime juice and coriander leaves. Add a splash of water to just cover the ingredients, if necessary, and leave to simmer for 2–3 minutes to cook the peas and blend the flavours. Taste and adjust the tamari sauce, if necessary. Tear over the basil leaves, if using, and it's ready to serve.

This is a straightforward Indo-Chinese recipe – cooked quite a bit in Indian households, but inspired by Chinese flavourings and stir-frying – and the combination of ginger, garlic and onion is always a good flavour builder. When I was younger, I worked at the Taipan Chinese restaurant at The Oberoi in New Delhi, and the staff meals were always vegetarian dishes like this. I worked with Chinese chefs then and they taught me a great deal about blending the two culinary cultures. Serve this with lots of sticky rice (page 284).

Vegetables in Chinese Curry Sauce

2 tablespoons sunflower oil
2.5cm piece of fresh ginger, peeled and finely chopped
4 garlic cloves, finely chopped
1 long, thin green chilli, thinly sliced
4 spring onions, finely chopped
100g brown cap mushrooms, trimmed and thinly sliced
1 carrot, peeled and thinly sliced
1 celery stick, thinly sliced
1 red onion, chopped
1 red pepper, cored, deseeded and chopped
1 courgette, halved lengthways and thinly sliced
500ml water
3 tablespoons sriracha hot chilli sauce
2 tablespoons tomato ketchup
2 teaspoons soy sauce, or to taste
1 tablespoon cornflour mixed with 2 tablespoons water to make a thin paste
sea salt and black pepper
chopped fresh coriander, to garnish

Heat a large wok that can be covered over a high heat. Add the oil and swirl it around. Add the ginger, garlic and green chilli, and stir-fry for 1 minute to flavour the oil and cook out the rawness from the ginger and garlic. Add the spring onions and continue stir-frying until they begin to soften.

Add the mushrooms, carrot, celery, red onion and red pepper, and continue stir-frying for several minutes until the carrots begin to soften. Add the courgette and season generously with freshly ground black pepper. Stir everything together.

Stir in the water, chilli sauce, ketchup and soy sauce. Now is the time to decide if you need to add salt. I haven't specified adding because of the amount of soy sauce in the recipe. Adjust the black pepper, if necessary.

Stir in the cornflour paste and bring to the boil, stirring constantly. Cover the wok, reduce the heat and simmer for about 10 minutes until all the vegetables are tender. Garnish with the chopped coriander and serve.

Some Chinese cooks use Madras curry powder to flavour their curries, while others look to Japan for their curry inspiration. I've used Japanese curry powder in this recipe. I hope you enjoy the contrast. Serve with sticky rice (page 284).

Chinese-style Vegetable & Tofu Curry

2 tablespoons cornflour
400g firm tofu, patted dry and
    cut into bite-sized pieces
groundnut or rapeseed oil
2 onions, thinly sliced
3 garlic cloves, finely chopped
1 long, thin green chilli
2 teaspoons Japanese curry
    powder (see page 56), or
    Madras curry powder, as mild
    or hot as you like
¼ teaspoon Chinese five-spice
    powder
¼ teaspoon ground cumin
½ teaspoon ground ginger
300g shiitake mushrooms,
    trimmed and quartered
800ml vegetable stock, ideally
    home-made (page 282)
2 tablespoons cornflour mixed
    with 4 tablespoons water
    to make a thin paste
1cm piece of fresh ginger,
    peeled and finely chopped
1 tablespoon soy sauce
150g small cauliflower florets
100g sugar-snap peas, trimmed
2 baby bok choy, trimmed,
    leaves separated, stacked
    and thinly sliced
1 tablespoon chilli paste
sea salt and freshly ground
    black pepper

Put the cornflour in a shallow bowl. Add the tofu, a few pieces at a time and toss to coat, then tap off any excess. Repeat until all pieces are coated. Line a plate with kitchen paper and set aside.

Heat a thin layer of oil in a wok with a lid over a medium-high heat. Add as many tofu pieces as will fit without overcrowding and fry until lightly coloured all over. Transfer to the lined plate and repeat until all the tofu is fried, adding a little more oil to the pan, if necessary. Stand back when you add the tofu, because, even if it has been well pressed, the water in it will splatter.

Wipe out the wok and return it to a high heat. Add 3 tablespoons oil and swirl it around. Add the onions with a pinch of salt and stir-fry until softened. Add the garlic and chilli and continue stir-frying until the onions are translucent. Add the curry powder, Chinese five-spice powder, ground cumin and ground ginger, and stir-fry for 30 seconds to cook the ground spices. Watch closely so nothing burns.

Add the mushrooms and continue stir-frying until they are coated in spices. Stir in the stock, cornflour paste, ginger and soy sauce, and bring to the boil. Add the cauliflower, cover and simmer for 7 minutes, or until the cauliflower is almost tender.

Add the sugar-snap peas and bok choy, re-cover and cook for about a further 3 minutes, or until all the vegetables are tender. Stir in the chilli paste and adjust the soy sauce, if necessary. It's ready to serve.

You might be surprised to see Madras curry powder in the list of ingredients for a Chinese recipe, but it often flavours dishes from southern China. The prepared powder that is sold in Chinese food stores is similar to the curry powder invented by the British during their time in India, and now known as Madras curry powder. This is what I have used here. Serve this ladled over rice noodles or sticky rice (page 284) for a meal in a bowl.

Tofu in Sweetcorn & Pepper Curry

groundnut or rapeseed oil
about 2 tablespoons cornflour
400g firm tofu, pressed (see Atul's tip, right), patted dry and cut into bite-sized pieces
1 carrot, peeled and finely diced
1 red pepper, cored, deseeded and finely chopped
75g frozen sweetcorn kernels
2 large handfuls bean sprouts, rinsed, plus extra to garnish

For the curry sauce
1½ tablespoons groundnut or rapeseed oil
3 garlic cloves, finely chopped
1 red onion, finely chopped
2 teaspoons Madras curry powder, mild or hot, as you like
1 teaspoon soft light brown sugar
500ml vegetable stock, ideally home-made (page 282)
2 celery sticks, trimmed and chopped
½ yellow pepper, cored, deseeded and chopped
1 tablespoon soy sauce

First, make the curry sauce. Heat a wok with a lid over a high heat. Add the oil and swirl it around. Add the garlic and stir-fry to flavour the oil. Add the onion and continue stir-frying until the onion is softened. Add the Madras curry powder and sugar and stir-fry for 30 seconds to cook the spices. Watch closely so the spices and sugar don't burn.

Pour in the stock, then add the celery, yellow pepper and soy sauce, and bring to the boil. Cover and leave to simmer for 15 minutes, or until the vegetables are very tender. Transfer the contents of the wok to a blender or food processor and process until a smooth sauce forms. Set aside.

Wash and dry the wok, then set aside. Line a baking tray or plate with kitchen paper.

Heat enough oil for deep-frying in a deep-fat fryer or heavy-based saucepan until it reaches 180°C. Put the cornflour in a shallow bowl. Add the tofu, a few pieces at a time, gently toss to coat, then tap off any excess cornflour. Repeat until all the tofu pieces are coated.

Add as many tofu pieces to the wok that will fit without overcrowding and deep-fry, turning over with a slotted spoon, until very lightly coloured. Transfer to the lined baking tray to drain. Continue

To garnish, optional
thinly sliced fresh red chilli
finely shredded coriander leaves
finely shredded spring onions

until all the tofu is fried, reheating the oil between batches, if necessary. Stand well back when you add the tofu, because even if it has been well pressed the water in it will still splutter.

Heat the wok over a high heat. Add 1 tablespoon oil and swirl it around. Add the carrot and red pepper and stir-fry until the carrot is almost tender. Add the sweetcorn kernels with the puréed curry sauce and stir together.

As the liquid begins to boil, stir in the tofu and continue boiling until the carrot, pepper and sweetcorn kernels are tender and the tofu is hot. Stir in the bean sprouts and let them warm through. Taste and adjust the soy sauce, if necessary. Garnish with the beansprouts, red chilli, coriander and spring onions, if using, and serve.

● atul's tip

You can buy tofu that comes pressed, ready for deep-frying, but with most brands it's important to remove the liquid before frying so the tofu doesn't fall apart in the hot oil. Tofu presses for this purpose are sold at most health food shops, or you can use two chopping boards. Line one board with a double layer of kitchen paper and place the block of tofu on top. Cover with another double layer of kitchen paper and the second chopping board. Put several cans of tomatoes or pulses on top to weigh down, and leave for 30 minutes. The liquid will be absorbed by the kitchen paper.

There aren't many experiences like sampling Singapore's street food for the first time! Influenced by the Chinese, Indians, Malaysians and Indonesians, it's an exciting mix of textures and flavours. Chilli crab is perhaps the best-known dish, and I think my vegan version holds its own.

Chilli 'Chicken'

sunflower oil

400g plant-based 'chicken' pieces

300ml vegetable stock, ideally home-made (page 282)

1 egg, beaten

1 tablespoon cornflour mixed with 3 tablespoons water

sea salt and freshly ground white pepper

spring onions, thinly sliced, to garnish

coriander leaves or microherbs, to garnish

sesame seeds, to garnish

For the sauce

3 tablespoons vegetable oil

2cm piece of fresh ginger, peeled and finely chopped

4–6 large fresh red chillies, to taste, deseeded and sliced

2 garlic cloves, finely chopped

1 large onion, chopped

2 tomatoes, finely diced

4 tablespoons sweet chilli sauce

1 tablespoon black bean sauce

4 tablespoons tomato ketchup

1 tablespoon toasted sesame oil

1 tablespoon soy sauce

1 tablespoon light brown sugar

1 teaspoon red chilli powder

1–2 teaspoons freshly ground white pepper, to taste

First, make the sauce. Heat a large dry wok over a high heat. Add the oil and swirl it around. Reduce the heat to medium-high, add the ginger, red chillies, garlic and onion, and stir-fry until fragrant and the onion is lightly coloured. Watch closely so the garlic and ginger don't burn.

Reduce to a low heat and add the tomatoes, chilli sauce, black bean sauce, ketchup, sesame oil, soy sauce, sugar, chilli powder and ground white pepper, stirring until the sugar dissolves. Simmer for 1–2 minutes for the flavours to blend. Remove from the heat and set aside while you cook the 'chicken' pieces.

Heat a thin layer of oil in a large frying pan over a low heat. Add as many 'chicken' pieces as will fit without overcrowding and fry, turning them over occasionally, until golden brown. Transfer to a tray lined with kitchen paper to drain while you fry the remaining pieces. You might have to top up the oil between batches.

Add the 'chicken' pieces and stock to the sauce. Turn on the heat under the wok and simmer for 1–2 minutes. Whisk the beaten egg and cornflour mixture together, then add to the wok and continue simmering, stirring all the time, until the sauce thickens. Taste and adjust the seasoning with extra soy sauce and/or white pepper. Garnish with spring onions, coriander and sesame seeds, and serve.

Mango is used in all forms in this part of the world, and both ripe and green mangoes are suitable for this recipe. (If you want to try this with green mangoes, the simmering time will increase about 20 minutes.) When the wonderfully sweet Alphonso mangoes are in season, give yourself a treat and grab four – this recipe stands out because of its sweet-and-sour character and fresh flavour. Serve this with jasmine rice (page 283) or basmati rice (page 283) and two other vegetables. I think cauliflower, roasted or stir-fried, is ideal. And, for something a bit different, try it with Twice-fried Spicy Cauliflower (page 16) from Korea.

Curried Mango
mangga kari

3 tablespoons rapeseed oil
1 teaspoon cumin seeds
3 garlic cloves, chopped
4 just-ripe mangoes, peeled and
    cut into wedges
150g grated jaggery or
    Demerara sugar
2 teaspoons red chilli powder
1½ teaspoons ground cumin
500ml hot water
sea salt
microherbs, to garnish

For the curry paste
150ml water
1 tablespoon Malay Curry
    Powder (page 274)
6 garlic cloves, crushed
2 tablespoons chopped
    coriander leaves

Mix all the ingredients for the curry paste together and set aside.

Heat a wok over a high heat. Add the oil and swirl it around. Reduce the heat, add the cumin seeds and garlic and stir-fry until the seeds crackle, but watch closely so the garlic doesn't burn. Stir in the curry paste and bring to the boil, then reduce the heat and continue stir-frying for 2 minutes. Stand back when you add the paste, because the water will splutter when it hits the hot oil.

Stir in the mango wedges, making sure they are well coated. Add the jaggery, chilli powder and ground cumin with salt to taste, and stir-fry for 30 seconds to cook the ground spices. Stir in the hot water, reduce the heat and leave to simmer, uncovered, for 10 minutes for just-ripe mangoes, or until the flesh is slightly soft. Remove the pan from the heat and serve the mangoes warm or at room temperature. Any leftovers will thicken after a day.

Left: Curried Mango (page 79)
Right: Chilli 'Chicken' (page 78)

africa

This is a seemingly simple soup is packed with richness from a perfectly fried egg and thick, creamy yogurt, along with the comforting flavours of saffron, paprika and cumin. It's an everyday Tunisian breakfast, but I think it's ideal for lunch or supper.

Chickpea Soup with Fried Eggs
lablabi

olive oil
2 onions, chopped
2 teaspoons ground cumin, plus
 a little extra for the fried eggs
4 garlic cloves, finely chopped
2 x 400g cans chickpeas, drained
 and rinsed
1 lemon, halved
a generous pinch of saffron
 powder
½ teaspoon black pepper
600ml vegetable stock, ideally
 home-made (page 282)
4 eggs
a pinch of smoked paprika, plus
 a little extra for the fried eggs
 and to garnish
sea salt

To serve
chopped flat-leaf parsley
full-fat natural yogurt
harissa
1 large radish, sliced, optional

Heat 4 tablespoons oil in a large saucepan with a lid over a medium-high heat. Add the onions and a pinch of salt and fry, stirring often, until the onions begin to soften. Add the ground cumin and stir for 30 seconds. Add the garlic and another pinch of salt and continue stirring until the onions start to turn light brown.

Stir in the chickpeas and squeeze in lemon juice to taste. Add the saffron powder, black pepper and stock, and bring to the boil. Reduce the heat slightly and leave to simmer while you fry the eggs.

Heat ½ teaspoon oil per egg in a frying pan, ideally non-stick, over a medium-high heat. When the oil is hot, carefully crack in the eggs and as soon as the whites lose their translucency sprinkle the yolks with the paprika, a pinch of cumin and salt to taste, and fry until the whites are perfectly set. If you are cooking the eggs in batches, transfer them to a plate and keep warm until all are cooked.

When you are ready to serve, return the soup to the boil, taste and adjust the seasoning, if necessary. Use the back of a large spoon or ladle to gently crush some of the chickpeas against the side of the pan to thicken the soup slightly. Ladle the soup into bowls, sprinkle with parsley and add a dollop of yogurt, harissa to taste, a few radish slices, if using, and a light dusting of paprika. Top each portion with a fried egg and another sprinkle of parsley and it's ready to serve. I put extra harissa on the table for everyone to help themselves if they want extra heat.

What a wonderfully versatile recipe this is. I was writing and testing this in the depth of winter when root vegetables are plentiful and at their best. During the rest of the year, use whatever is available, including potatoes and/or kohlrabi – you just need a total of about 500g prepared vegetables. You can also replace the lentils with just about any pulse in your cupboard; chickpeas, butter beans and kidney beans would all be equally good. I serve this with slices of baguette or flatbreads, and Arab pickles on the side are good, too.

Root Vegetable & Lentil Stew
mehalta

3 tablespoons olive oil
1 onion, chopped
1 tablespoon harissa
1½ teaspoons *baharat*
  (page 276)
1 teaspoon ground cumin
1 teaspoon sweet paprika
100g peeled carrot, chopped
100g peeled celeriac, chopped
100g peeled parsnip, chopped
100g peeled swede, chopped
1 tablespoon mixed chopped
  coriander and flat-leaf parsley,
  plus an extra handful each,
  to garnish
1.5cm piece of fresh ginger,
  peeled and chopped
4 garlic cloves, chopped
½ teaspoon ground
  black pepper
100g cauliflower florets
vegetable stock, ideally home
  made (page 282)
2 x 400g cans green lentils,
  drained
200g spinach leaves, chopped
  and rinsed
sea salt

Heat the oil in a large saucepan with a lid over a medium-high heat. Add the onion with a pinch of salt and fry, stirring often, until the onion is translucent. Stir in the harissa, *baharat*, ground cumin and paprika, and fry for 30 seconds to cook the ground spices.

Add all the root vegetables and the chopped herbs with salt to taste. Give it all a good stir, then add the ginger, garlic and black pepper, and continue frying for about 1 minute. Stir in the cauliflower florets.

Pour over enough vegetable stock to cover the vegetables. Cover the pan and bring to the boil. Reduce the heat, partially uncover the pan and leave to simmer for 20 minutes, or until all the vegetables are tender.

Stir in the lentils and return the stew to the boil, then stir in the spinach leaves. When the spinach wilts, taste and adjust the salt and pepper, if necessary. Sprinkle generously with chopped coriander and parsley just before serving.

This is one of the most common dishes across all of North Africa, which, although I've called it a soup, is so hearty you wouldn't be wrong to call it a stew. Flavoured with harissa and ground cumin, the chickpeas and green lentils make this filling and nutritious.

Spiced Vegetable & Mixed Pulse Soup
harira

4 tablespoons olive oil
200g carrots, peeled and diced
200g celery, diced
1 red onion, finely chopped
1 teaspoon ground toasted cumin seeds (page 270)
1 teaspoon harissa, plus extra to serve
½ teaspoon ground turmeric
1 can (400g) chopped tomatoes
40g mixed coriander and flat-leaf parsley leaves, finely chopped, plus extra to garnish
1 litre vegetable stock, simmering, ideally home-made (page 282)
200g dried green lentils, rinsed
1 can (400g) chickpeas, drained and rinsed
sea salt and freshly ground black pepper

To thicken
500ml water
1 egg
1 tablespoon plain flour
4 tablespoons freshly squeezed lemon juice

Heat the oil in a large saucepan with a lid over a medium-high heat. Add the carrots, celery and red onion with a pinch of salt, and fry, stirring often, until the onion is translucent. The salt helps to cook the onion and bring the flavours out of the carrot and celery. Add the ground cumin seeds, harissa and turmeric, and stir for 30 seconds to cook the ground spices.

Add the tomatoes – swirl the can with a little water to get all the juices out – the mixed coriander and parsley and salt to taste, then stir together for a minute or so. Stir in the vegetable stock and lentils and bring to the boil. Cover the pan, reduce the heat and leave to simmer for 30 minutes or until the lentils are tender – you should be able to crush them between your fingertips.

Stir in the chickpeas with a pinch of black pepper and leave the soup bubbling on the side.

To thicken, pour the water into a saucepan, then add the egg and flour with a pinch of black pepper. Using a balloon whisk, whisk together until the flour is combined, then add the lemon juice. Cook over a medium heat, whisking constantly, until the mixture thickens. Pour the egg mixture into the bubbling soup, stir and return to the boil, stirring.

Taste and adjust the salt and pepper, if necessary. Garnish with coriander and flat-leaf parsley and serve with extra harissa on the table for anyone who wants more of a chilli kick.

Fresh herbs, garlic, lemon juice and warming spices are the ingredients you'd expect to find in a traditional chermoula sauce, popular in Morocco and throughout North Africa. In this recipe, however, I've created a honey-sweetened version and omitted chilli powder, which you might expect – I like to let the magic of garlic, lemon and honey to come through. Chermoula is typically served with meat or seafood, but it's a perfect accompaniment for a whole roasted cauliflower.

Chermoula Cauliflower
chermoula qarnabit

1 large head of cauliflower, trimmed and left whole
sea salt

For the chermoula sauce
3 garlic cloves, crushed
4 tablespoons olive oil
4 tablespoons runny honey
1 tablespoon ground toasted cumin seeds (page 270)
1 tablespoon smoked paprika
½ teaspoon ground black pepper
finely grated zest of 1 large lemon
4 tablespoons freshly squeezed lemon juice
30–40g fresh coriander leaves, chopped
slivered almonds, toasted, to garnish
lettuce leaves on the side, to garnish

Preheat the oven to 200°C/Fan 180°C/Gas 6 and line a roasting pan with baking paper, making sure the baking comes up the side of the pan.

To make the chermoula sauce, combine the garlic, olive oil, honey, ground cumin seeds, paprika, black pepper, lemon zest and a pinch of salt in a large bowl. Whisk in the lemon juice, then add about three-quarters of the coriander leaves.

Place the cauliflower upside-down in the bowl and spoon over the chermoula sauce. Use your hands to rub the sauce all over the cauliflower, top and bottom, making sure it goes between the florets. Push any leftover sauce into the gap between the central core and florets on the bottom – you don't want to lose any of that flavour.

Transfer the cauliflower, right-side up, to the roasting pan. Pour over any sauce remaining in the bowl and cover with foil, pressing the foil around the cauliflower. Place in the oven and roast for 30 minutes.

Uncover the pan and continue roasting for a further 25 minutes, or until it the cauliflower is tender and slightly charred. You should be able to slide a knife into the core easily. Sprinkle with the remaining coriander leaves and serve.

Essentially North African, this dish appears in many guises throughout the continent and the Middle East, particularly as a breakfast dish. The one consistent ingredient is eggs, which you can cook as firm or soft as you like. This recipe stays true to tradition, but I've spiced up the vegetable mixture with *baharat*, the Middle Eastern spice powder. I think this is perfect for a lazy weekend breakfast. I serve it with thick Greek yogurt, toasted pitta breads or sliced baguette and a pot of harissa on the table.

Shakshuka

2 tablespoons olive oil
2 garlic cloves, finely chopped
2 onions, chopped
1 teaspoon *baharat* (page 276)
1 teaspoon ground coriander
1 teaspoon ground cumin
1 teaspoon hot paprika
6 tomatoes, chopped
1 green pepper, cored,
  deseeded and thinly sliced
1 red pepper, cored, deseeded
  and thinly sliced
2 tablespoons chopped flat-leaf
  parsley leaves
1 tablespoon chopped
  oregano leaves
8 eggs
sea salt and freshly ground
  black pepper
chopped coriander, to garnish

Heat the oil in a large frying pan with a lid over a medium-high heat. Add the garlic and onions and fry, stirring, until the onion softens. Add the *baharat*, ground coriander, ground cumin and paprika, and stir for 30 seconds to cook the ground spices. Watch closely so nothing catches and burns.

Stir in the tomatoes, green and red peppers, parsley and oregano with salt and pepper to taste. Stir until the tomatoes start to break down, then reduce the heat to low, and leave the vegetables to simmer for 15 minutes or until very tender.

Taste the vegetables and adjust the salt and pepper, if necessary. Use the back of your spoon to make 8 wells in the surface. Crack an egg into each well. Cover the pan and leave to simmer over a low heat for 4–5 minutes for a soft-cooked eggs. Garnish with chopped coriander and serve with plenty of bread, harissa and thick, creamy yogurt on the side.

Although this stews gets its punchy flavour from a classic Algerian chilli paste, it reminds me of an everyday Indian family dish – it's simple and filling, and goes well with quickly stir-fried green vegetables and a bowl of brown basmati rice (page 283). For variety, replace the potatoes with sweet potatoes or jackfruit.

Spicy Potato Stew
chtitha batata

1 tablespoon olive oil
600g floury potatoes, such
    as King Edwards, peeled and
    cut into bite-sized pieces
125ml passata, or 2 tablespoons
    tomato paste dissolved in
    125ml water
sea salt
chopped coriander leaves,
    to garnish

**For the *dersa* paste (Algerian
    chilli paste)**
1 tablespoon olive oil
4 garlic cloves, peeled
1 long, thin green chilli, chopped
1 teaspoon cumin seeds
1 teaspoon hot paprika
½ teaspoon black pepper
½ teaspoon cayenne pepper
a pinch of sea salt

First, make the *dersa* paste. Put the olive oil, garlic cloves, green chilli, cumin seeds, paprika, black pepper, cayenne pepper and salt in a spice grinder, coffee grinder or small food processor, and grind until a coarse paste forms, scraping down the side of the bowl as necessary.

Heat the olive oil in a large, deep frying pan over a medium-high heat. Add the *dersa* paste and fry, stirring, for 1 minute to cook the garlic. It becomes very fragrant as it fries.

Add the potatoes and stir until they are well coated in the paste. Stir in the passata, salt to taste and just enough water to cover the potatoes. Bring to the boil, then reduce the heat and leave to simmer, uncovered, for 30–40 minutes, stirring occasionally, until the potatoes are tender. As the liquid evaporates, watch closely so the potatoes don't stick and burn. Taste and adjust the salt, if necessary. Garnish with coriander leaves and serve.

I've put this nutritional recipe in the Kenyan section, but in all honesty it's a popular dish all over the African continent – it's quick and easy, and inexpensive. The nutrients in the beans and sweetcorn complement each other to make a complete amino acid, essential for a healthy body, which can be lacking in vegetarian and vegan diets. Serve this with rice or bread.

Sweetcorn & Kidney Bean Curry
gilteri

1 tablespoon sunflower oil
1 red onion, finely chopped
2 garlic cloves, chopped
½ long, thin green chilli, chopped
1 teaspoon East African Curry Powder (page 273)
½ teaspoon smoked paprika
250ml water
150g frozen sweetcorn kernels
1 can (400g) red kidney beans, drained and rinsed
¼ can (100g) chopped tomatoes
sea salt
chopped coriander leaves, to garnish
spring onions cut into julienne slices, to garnish

Heat the oil in a saucepan over a medium-high heat. Add the onion and fry, stirring occasionally, until it is softened. Add the garlic and green chilli and stir around, then add the curry powder and paprika and stir for 30 seconds to cook the spices. Watch closely so they do not burn.

Add the water, sweetcorn kernels, kidney beans and chopped tomatoes with salt to taste, and stir together. Bring to the boil, then lower the heat and leave to simmer, uncovered, for 10 minutes to blend the flavours and reduce the liquid.

Taste and adjust the salt, if necessary. Spoon into bowls and garnish with coriander and spring onions.

Paneer isn't an indigenous African ingredient, but there is a large Gujarati community in Kenya, which is why I've included this simple recipe here. Typically, Gujarati cooking is flavoured with ginger and chilli powder and you get both in the East African Curry Powder.

Swahili Paneer Curry

2 tablespoons sunflower oil
1 large onion, finely chopped
2 garlic cloves, chopped
2.5cm piece of fresh ginger, peeled and chopped
½ *each* green, red and yellow peppers, cored, deseeded and cut into bite-sized pieces
2 tablespoons East African Curry Powder (page 273)
3 tomatoes, chopped
200g paneer, cut into bite-sized pieces (see Atul's tip, below)
4 tablespoons passata
125ml coconut milk
125ml water
sea salt

To finish
5 tablespoons coconut milk, optional
1 long, thin green chilli, finely chopped or halved
chopped coriander leaves
½ lemon

Heat the oil in a saucepan over a medium-high heat. Add the onion with a pinch of salt and fry, stirring often, until softened. Add the garlic and ginger and stir for 1 minute to cook out the rawness. Add the mixed peppers and continue stirring until they begin to soften.

Add the curry powder and stir for 30 seconds. Add the tomatoes and give them a good stir, then stir in the paneer and passata. Stir in the coconut milk and water, turn up the heat and bring to the boil. Reduce the heat and leave to simmer, uncovered, for 10 minutes to concentrate the flavours and reduce. Taste and adjust the salt, if necessary.

When ready to serve, spoon the 5 tablespoons coconut milk over, if using. Garnish with the green chilli and coriander leaves and squeeze in lemon juice to taste to cut through the richness.

atul's tip

For a vegan option, replace the paneer with chopped firm tofu.

This vegan classic from Nairobi makes a perfect one-pot meal, with a fantastic rich, creamy coconut sauce that has a hint of a kick from the green chilli. Gujarati immigrants have settled throughout Africa, especially in Kenya, so there is a blending of both culinary traditions, and this recipe comes from that hybrid.

Pigeon Pea & Coconut Curry
bherzai

2 tablespoons sunflower oil, olive oil or coconut oil
¼ teaspoon cumin seeds
seeds from ½ green cardamom pod
1 onion, finely chopped
1 garlic clove, chopped
0.5cm piece of fresh ginger, peeled and finely chopped
1½ teaspoons ground coriander
½ teaspoon ground turmeric
200g frozen pigeon or gungo peas (see Atul's tip, below)
300ml coconut milk
300ml water
1 teaspoon finely chopped green chilli
sea salt
coriander leaves, to garnish
finely sliced red onion, to garnish

Heat the oil in a saucepan over a medium-high heat. Add the cumin and cardamom seeds, and stir until they crackle. Add the onion with 1 teaspoon salt and fry, stirring often, until the onion is light brown.

Add the garlic and ginger and continue stirring for 1 minute to cook out the rawness. Watch that they do not burn. Add the ground coriander and turmeric and continue stirring for 30 seconds to cook the ground spices. Add a splash of water, if necessary, to stop everything sticking to the bottom of the pan.

Add the pigeon peas, coconut milk, water and green chilli, and stir together. Bring to the boil, reduce the heat and leave to simmer for 3–4 minutes until the pigeon peas are cooked and the sauce thickened. Taste and adjust the salt, if necessary. Garnish with coriander and red onion just before serving.

atul's tip

This dish is traditionally made with gungo peas, but frozen pigeon peas are a good alternative. If you'd rather use dried pigeon or gungo peas, rinse them well and soak in water for 20 minutes. Drain and cook according to the packet instructions, then drain again and add at the same place in the recipe.

Indian workers in Kenya often form local clubs where they meet at the end of the day for drinks and camaraderie, and spiced-up chips like these are a popular snack. Whenever I think of Kenyan food, the three dominant flavours of cumin, coriander and red chillies immediately rush to my palate. These are three flavours that I think work incredibly well together, and they are what I'm using here – along with mango powder and lemon juice for a spicy-sour combination.

Kenyan Masala Chips

600g oven-baked chips
3 tablespoons sunflower oil
1 garlic clove, chopped
½ fresh red chilli, chopped
1 teaspoon cumin seeds
1 red onion, finely chopped
2 teaspoons ground coriander
2 teaspoons mango powder (*amchur*), plus a little extra for dusting, or use lemon juice
½ teaspoon ground cumin
¼ teaspoon ground turmeric
2 tomatoes, chopped
4 tablespoons passata
½ lemon
about 2 tablespoons chopped coriander leaves, plus extra to garnish
red chilli powder for dusting
sea salt

Preheat the oven and cook the oven chips according to the packet instructions until golden brown and crisp. Keep hot.

Meanwhile, heat the oil in a large saucepan over a medium-high heat. Add the garlic, red chilli and cumin seeds, and stir until the seeds crackle. Add the red onion and fry, stirring often, until it softens. Add the ground coriander, mango powder, ground cumin and turmeric, and stir for 30 seconds to cook the spices.

Stir in the tomatoes with a pinch of salt and keep stirring until the onions soften and the tomatoes start to break down. You've got to watch closely so the onions don't catch on the bottom of the pan. As soon as you think they might be catching, stir in the passata to keep the mixture moist. Squeeze in 4 teaspoons lemon juice, or to taste. If you are using lemon juice instead of mango powder, now is the time to add extra. Adjust the salt, if necessary.

Add the chips to the pan along with the coriander leaves and a very light dusting of chilli powder and mango powder, then gently mix together. Garnish with a little extra chopped coriander and serve.

Left: Pigeon Pea &
Coconut Curry (page 96)
Right: Kenyan Masala
Chips (page 97)

Universally acknowledged as Egypt's national dish, this is meal-on-a plate is traditionally served on its own – not surprising, as it's a filling dish with pasta *and* rice *and* pulses. If you want to stretch this recipe to feed a few more friends, add a Middle Eastern chopped salad and it will serve 8 as a sharing dish.

Rice, Beans & Pasta
koshari

sunflower oil
120g dried pasta, such as fusilli
 or macaroni
400g white basmati rice, rinsed
 under cold running water until
 the water runs clear and then
 soaked in fresh cold water
 to cover for 30 minutes
1 onion, finely chopped
4 garlic cloves, finely chopped
2 teaspoons ground coriander
1 teaspoon ground cumin, plus
 a little extra for the pasta
1 teaspoon sweet paprika, plus
 a little extra for the pasta
½ teaspoon red chilli flakes
2 tablespoons white wine vinegar
500ml passata
500ml water
1 can (400g) green lentils,
 drained and rinsed
1 can (400g) chickpeas, drained
 and rinsed
4 tablespoons chopped flat-leaf
 parsley leaves, plus extra
 to garnish
1 lemon, halved, or to taste
sea salt

First, fry the onion rings for the garnish (see Atul's tip, right). Put the sliced onion, rice flour and chilli powder in a bowl and toss together. Heat a 0.5cm layer of oil in a large frying pan over a high heat until a piece of onion sizzles when added to the hot oil. Add as many onion rings as will fit in a single layer and fry, turning them over regularly, until golden brown on each side. Transfer them to a plate lined with kitchen paper to drain, then continue until all the slices are fried. You might have to replenish and/or reheat the oil between batches.

Next, cook the pasta. Bring a saucepan of salted water to the boil. Add the pasta and boil, following the packet instructions, until al dente. Drain well and rinse under cold water to stop the cooking. Toss it with just a little oil to prevent sticking, then set aside.

Meanwhile, drain the rice and set aside.

Heat 2 tablespoons oil in a flameproof casserole or large saucepan with a lid over a medium-high heat. Add the chopped onion with a pinch of salt, and fry, stirring often, until the onion turns light brown. Add the garlic, ground coriander, ground cumin, paprika and chilli flakes, and stir for 30 seconds to cook the ground spices. Add the vinegar and stir, scraping up any brown bits from the base of the pan.

To garnish

1 small onion, very thinly sliced
into rings

1 tablespoon rice flour

¼ teaspoon red chilli powder

Add the passata and water and bring to the boil. Add the drained rice, lentils and salt to taste. Place a double layer of baking paper on top of the rice and lentils and drizzle over water to just moisten the paper. Cover the casserole with the lid and leave to gently cook for 10 minutes, or until the rice is tender with separate fluffy grains and there isn't any liquid on the bottom of the pan. Don't take the lid off to check under the paper before it has simmered for 10 minutes.

Meanwhile, heat 1 tablespoon oil in a large frying pan over a medium-high heat. Add the cooked pasta and chickpeas with a pinch each of ground cumin and paprika and salt to taste, and stir together. Stir in half the parsley.

Remove the paper from the cooked rice and fluff the rice and lentils with a fork. Tip the pasta and chickpeas into the casserole and squeeze over the lemon halves. Add the remaining chopped parsley and stir everything together. Serve this on a large platter, garnished with the onion rings and extra chopped parsley.

atul's tip

Fried onions are an essential garnish, but a time-consuming part of the recipe. In professional kitchens we buy deep-fried onion rings to save on time and the expense of using the oil only once. So, if you see any, go ahead and grab them. If you do fry the onion rings, save the oil and use it to sauté the pasta and chickpeas in the recipe.

Serves 4

Okra has been a staple Egyptian ingredient since ancient times, and most Egyptians grow up eating this simple, nutritious okra dish with a spiced tomato base. It's particularly warming in the winter months. In this version, I use soya mince to replace the traditional main ingredient. Freshly cooked basmati rice (page 283) and pitta bread are natural partners, and I think it also goes well a mixture of wholemeal vermicelli and bulgar wheat, which you can find in Middle Eastern food shops.

Okra Stew
bamya

30g dried soya mince or 125g rehydrated soya mince
2½ tablespoons olive oil
1 large red onion, chopped
4 garlic cloves, finely chopped
250g okra pods, stem ends removed and the pods chopped
300ml passata
150ml water
1½ tablespoons freshly squeezed lemon juice
1¼ teaspoons ground cumin
1¼ teaspoons sweet paprika
¾ teaspoon ground black pepper
½ teaspoon sugar
2½ tablespoons chopped coriander leaves
sea salt

If using dried soya mince, soak the mince in freshly boiled water to cover for 15 minutes, or until tender and spongy. Drain and rinse it under running cold water, then leave it to sit in the sieve to let the excess water drain away.

Heat the oil in a large saucepan with a lid over a medium-high heat. Add the onion and fry, stirring. Add the garlic and a pinch of salt and continue stirring until the onion is softened. Stir in the okra, then add the passata, water and lemon juice, and bring to the boil. Stir in the cumin, paprika, black pepper and sugar.

Add the soya mince with salt to taste, and make sure everything is well mixed. Reduce the heat, cover the pan and leave to simmer, stirring occasionally, for 15 minutes, or until the okra is tender. Taste and adjust the salt, if necessary. Stir in the coriander and it's ready to serve.

I'd never cooked with a spice mixture quite like the berbere spice powder in this recipe before, and I absolutely loved it. The dish smells amazing as it's cooking, and I can honestly say this is one of the best curries I have ever made. As well as tasting so delicious, this recipe also incredibly versatile in that you can add just about any vegetable you like. (Jackfruit doesn't grow in Ethiopia, but if you want to experiment and go a bit off-piste, I think it would be fantastic in this recipe.) Red rice is the traditional accompaniment, often enriched with a little peanut butter stirred in. Otherwise, I suggest you serve this with freshly boiled basmati rice (page 283) and Ethiopian flatbreads – *injera* is a traditional fermented flatbread.

Berbere Vegetable Curry

2 tablespoons coconut oil
1 large red onion, halved and thinly sliced
1 tablespoon Berbere Spice Powder (page 276)
150g frozen peas
150g baby plum tomatoes, halved
150g mangetout, halved crosswise
400ml coconut milk
1 or 2 fresh red bird's-eye chillies, to taste
100g small broccoli florets
1 can (400g) chopped tomatoes
sea salt

Melt the coconut oil in a large saucepan with a lid over a medium-high heat. Add the onion with a pinch of salt and fry, stirring often, until the onion is starting to soften. Reduce the heat to medium and stir in the Berbere spice powder, stirring until well combined.

Add the peas, halved tomatoes and mangetout, and stir together. Add the coconut milk, red chillies, broccoli florets and chopped tomatoes, and bring to the boil, stirring. Reduce the heat, cover the pan and leave to simmer for 5–7 minutes until all the vegetables are tender.

Taste and adjust the salt, if necessary, but note the onions were salted and the spice powder contains salt, so you might not need much. It's ready to serve.

I haven't eaten a lot of Ethiopian food, but when I have it's always been thoroughly enjoyable – this dish always makes me want to return to a favourite north London restaurant. I love this, and I hope you do, too. I've always said that fat is a wonderful carrier of flavours, and that is exactly what the highly flavoured Ethiopian spice butter does – it imparts a rich, spiced flavour to any ingredients cooked with it, really lifting this simple lentil stew to a higher level. All the impurities in the butter are removed by the slow cooking, so the butter can then be cooked at a high temperature, exactly like using ghee or plain clarified butter.

Spiced Red Lentil Stew
misir wat

200g split red lentils (*masoor daal*), rinsed and soaked in cold water to cover for 20 minutes
Ethiopian Spiced Butter (below)
1 onion, finely chopped
3 garlic cloves, finely chopped
1 large tomato, chopped – use a very ripe one for this
2 tablespoons Berbere Spice Powder (page 276)
1 tablespoon tomato purée
350ml vegetable stock, ideally home-made (page 282)
sea salt
chopped coriander and/or flat-leaf parsley leaves, to garnish

For the Ethiopian Spiced Butter (*niter kibbeh*)
120g butter, chopped
3 garlic cloves, finely chopped
1.5cm piece fresh ginger, peeled and chopped

First, make the spiced butter. Put the butter and all the remaining ingredients in a heavy-based saucepan over a low heat, stirring until the butter melts. Leave it to simmer for about 2 minutes until a thick froth appears. Keep stirring and watching closely so the butter doesn't burn, which can happen very quickly. When the froth separates from the golden clear liquid and the sediment settles at the bottom, it's time to strain the butter. Use your spoon to press down on the flavourings to extract all the flavour they have to give. Set aside.

Drain the lentils and set aside.

Set aside 1 tablespoon of the spiced butter, then heat the remainder in a saucepan with a lid over a high heat. Add the onion with a pinch of salt and fry, stirring often, until the onion is light golden brown.

Reduce the heat slightly, add the garlic, chopped tomato, spice powder and tomato purée, and continue frying for 1 minute, stirring constantly. You've got to cook the tomato purée at this point, or it can taste too sour in the finished dish.

2 black cardamom pods, bruised

1 dried bay leaf

2 tablespoons finely chopped shallots

1 teaspoon coriander seeds

1 teaspoon cumin seeds

1 teaspoon fenugreek seeds

¼ teaspoon black peppercorns

several shards of cinnamon bark

Stir the lentils into the pan, then add the vegetable stock and a little salt, to taste. Bring to the boil, partially cover the pan and leave to simmer for 25 minutes, or until the lentils are very tender. Watch closely towards the end of cooking and stir to prevent the mixture sticking to the bottom of the pan. Tomatoes slow down the lentil cooking, so this might take a bit longer than you expect.

Taste and adjust the salt, if necessary. Drizzle with the remaining melted spiced butter and serve sprinkled with chopped coriander and/or parsley leaves to garnish.

Makes 8

This is Ugandan street food that gives you a vegetarian meal on the go in a wrap. If you say 'rolled eggs' repeatedly very quickly, you can hear how the name 'rolex' evolved in the local dialect. This is good for lunch at your desk, to take on a picnic or for a weekend brunch. I've given you the list of the ingredients I used for the filling, but feel free to substitute any vegetable you like eating raw, or add a little grated paneer or crumbled tofu, if you like. You get a great texture contrast for the soft omelette and the crunchy vegetable filling.

Rolled Egg Wraps
rolexs

3 eggs
1 tablespoon finely shredded
  coriander leaves
¼ teaspoon red chilli powder
½ teaspoon ground turmeric
sunflower oil
4 tablespoons finely shredded
  cabbage
4 tablespoons peeled and finely
  grated carrots
4 tablespoons finely chopped
  red onion
sea salt

For the bread wraps
140g plain white, plain
  wholemeal or chapati (*atta*)
  flour, plus extra for dusting
125ml water
½ thin, long green chilli, finely
  chopped
4 tablespoons finely shredded
  coriander leaves
1 teaspoon peeled and very
  finely chopped fresh ginger
½ tablespoon sunflower oil

First, make the dough for the bread wraps. Put the flour in a bowl with a pinch of salt and make a well in the centre. Add the water, green chilli, coriander leaves and ginger, and mix together to make a soft dough. Knead in the oil and roll the dough into a ball. Set aside while making the omelettes.

Break the eggs into a bowl and add the coriander leaves, red chilli powder, turmeric and a pinch of salt, and whisk together.

Heat a thin layer of oil in a large, non-stick frying pan over a medium-high heat. Add 1 tablespoon cabbage, carrot and red onion, and fry, stirring, until the vegetables are tender. Pour in one-quarter of the egg mixture and fry until the omelette is set on the bottom. Move the eggs around the pan, pushing out the uncooked mixture from the centre so the omelette sets evenly. When you can run a spatula around the egg and lift the omelette, slide it on to a plate. Continue to make 3 more omelettes, adding more oil to the pan between each, if necessary. Set aside.

Wash and dry the pan to use it for making the flatbreads for the wraps. Lightly dust your work surface with flour and put some flour in a small

For the filling
red cabbage, finely shredded
spring onion, finely shredded
baby spinach leaves, rinsed and
    patted dry
red onion, finely chopped
bottled chilli sauce

bowl. Divide the dough into 4 equal pieces and form each into a ball. Working with one dough ball at a time, press it into the bowl of flour, so it's coated on both sides. Roll out each ball on a floured surface into a thin circle, about 20cm across. You want it to be roughly the same size as the omelettes. Flip it back and forth between your hands to remove any excess flour.

Reheat the pan over a medium-high heat until very hot. One at a time, slap a dough circle on to the pan and dry-fry for 1 minute, or until it starts to bubble and brown specks appear on the underside. Flip it over and repeat. Brush the top with a little oil, turn over again and continue cooking for a further minute, or until the bread is light brown (see Atul's tip, below). Brush with very little oil and flip over one final time. Transfer the flatbread to a tray or plate lined with kitchen paper, cover with a cloth and keep hot, if serving warm, until you are ready to assemble.

To assemble, place a flatbread on a plate and top with an omelette. Add the red cabbage, spring onions and spinach leaves along the centre of the omelette. Sprinkle with red onion and drizzle with chilli sauce. Roll the bread wrap and omelette up and over the fillings, to make a tight cylinder, as if you were rolling a filled Swiss roll. Wrap in greaseproof paper, then cut in half. Continue to assemble 3 more wraps.

● atul's tip

The key to making these wraps is to cook the breads very well on both sides. If the bread is not properly cooked all the way through, eating raw dough can be a very unpleasant experience. One obvious short-cut for this recipe is to replace the home-made flatbreads with soft flour tortillas.

Serves 4

I've added broccoli and parboiled potatoes to this thick and rich stew, but as long as it contains sweetcorn and coconut you can pretty much add any vegetables you like and still have an authentic dish. In this recipe I've included both toasted sweetcorn kernels and sliced corn cobs for variety. In Uganda, this would be served with a pile of East African chapatis, but any soft flatbread will do, as long as you can use it to pick up the corn cob slices with your fingers. (Or, spear the pieces with a fork and eat the kernels that way.) This is messy, but delicious.

Sweetcorn in Coconut Stew
kasodi

2 floury potatoes, such as King Edwards, peeled and halved
100g frozen sweetcorn kernels
145g unsalted skinned peanuts
2 corn cobs, husked and halved crossways
1½ tablespoons sunflower oil
¼ teaspoon asafoetida
1.5cm piece of fresh ginger, peeled and finely chopped
1 long, thin green chilli, finely chopped
1 teaspoon cumin seeds
500ml passata
2½ teaspoons ground coriander
½ teaspoon ground turmeric
400ml coconut milk
70g small broccoli florets
sea salt
chopped coriander leaves, to garnish
spring onion thinly sliced, to garnish
chapatis or other soft flatbreads, to serve

Put the potatoes in a saucepan with a lid and add enough water to cover, along with a good pinch of salt. Cover the pan and bring to the boil, then boil for 20–25 minutes until the potatoes are tender. Drain well and rinse under cold running water. When cool enough to handle, cut into bite-sized pieces. Set aside.

Meanwhile, put the sweetcorn kernels in a dry frying pan over a high heat and fry, stirring occasionally, until the kernels thaw, are lightly coloured and begin to pop. Any liquid that comes from the kernels will evaporate. Watch closely so none of the kernels burn. Set aside.

Put the peanuts in a dry frying pan over a medium-high heat and stir until lightly browned and starting to pop. Quickly tip them out of the pan and leave to cool, then transfer to a food processor and process until coarsely ground. Set aside.

Put the corn cobs in a separate pan of boiling salted water and boil for 8 minutes, or until tender. Drain well and rinse under cold water to stop the cooking. Cut each half into 2cm-thick slices and set aside.

When you're ready to cook the stew, heat the oil in a large saucepan over a medium-high heat. Add the asafoetida and stir until it foams and subsides. Add the ginger, green chilli and cumin seeds, and fry, stirring, until the seeds crackle. Stir in the passata and ground peanuts and leave to simmer, stirring occasionally, for 2–3 minutes until the peanuts start to thicken the mixture.

Add the ground coriander, turmeric and salt to taste, and stir for 30 seconds to cook the spices. Stir in the coconut milk and leave to simmer, uncovered and stirring occasionally, for about 5 minutes to blend the flavours.

Stir the toasted sweetcorn kernels and broccoli florets into the stew and leave them to simmer, uncovered, until the broccoli is just tender. Stir in the corn cob slices and warm through. Add the potato pieces at the last minute to reheat, because they are already quite soft. Taste and adjust the salt, if necessary. Garnish with the coriander leaves and sliced spring onion and serve with plenty of flatbreads.

What I like about cooking with mushrooms is how they soak up flavours. I've suggested button mushrooms here, but go ahead and experiment with chestnut, oyster, shiitake, Portobello mushrooms or any variety you find. Each has a different flavour and adds a different texture – chunky Portobellos make this dish more substantial. The richness in this dish comes from the red pepper, and the heat from the curry powder. Chapatis (page 288) are ideal to serve with this simple curry.

Mushroom Curry
uyoga kari

2 tablespoons sunflower oil
1 onion, chopped
2 garlic cloves, chopped
1 tablespoon East African Curry Powder (page 273)
4 tablespoons passata
½ red pepper, cored, deseeded and finely chopped
400g button mushrooms, stalks removed with the caps left whole
125ml coconut milk
1 tablespoon freshly squeezed lemon juice
sea salt
chopped coriander, to garnish
chopped red chilli, to garnish

Heat the oil in a saucepan over a medium-high heat. Add the onion and fry, stirring often, until it is light brown. Add the garlic and curry powder and stir for 1 minute to cook the spices and the garlic. Watch closely so the curry powder does not burn. Stir in the passata and red pepper. I think the pepper adds a nice richness.

Add the mushrooms with salt to taste and stir so they are coated in the tomato mixture. Add the coconut milk and bring to the boil. If you think the texture is too thick, stir in a little extra water. At this point, lower the heat a little and leave the mushrooms to simmer for 7–10 minutes until they are tender.

Just before serving, add the lemon juice and adjust the salt, if necessary. Garnish with coriander and chopped red chilli and serve.

This is a good side dish to serve as part of any African meal. For a pan-African mix, I think this goes especially well with Sweetcorn and Kidney Bean Curry (page 93) and/or Kasodi (page 114). Add a bowl of freshly boiled basmati rice (page 283) and chapatis (page 288) or naans (page 287) and I think you will greatly enjoy it.

Stewed Broccoli & Cauliflower
biligani la kukaanga

2 tablespoons sunflower oil
½ teaspoon fenugreek seeds
½ teaspoon black onion seeds (nigella)
1 onion, chopped
1 tomato, halved and thinly sliced
2 teaspoons East African Curry Powder (page 273)
½ teaspoon mango powder (*amchur*), or use lemon juice
100g broccoli florets
100g cauliflower florets
250ml vegetable stock, ideally home-made (page 282) or water
sea salt
chopped coriander leaves, to serve

Heat the oil in a large saucepan with a lid over a medium-high heat. Add the fenugreek seeds and onion seeds and fry, stirring, until the seeds darken and pop. Add the onion with a pinch of salt and fry, stirring often, until it turns translucent. Stir in the tomato, then add the curry powder and mango powder and continue stirring for 30 seconds to cook the spices in the curry powder.

Add the broccoli and cauliflower florets with salt to taste and stir them into the onion and tomato mixture. Add the vegetable stock, cover the pan and leave the vegetables to simmer for 7–10 minutes until tender. Taste and adjust the salt, if necessary, and if you are using lemon juice rather than mango powder, now is the time to add. Sprinkle with coriander and serve.

This is a recipe I expect to end up on the menu of one of my restaurants. I always like to have an interesting mash dish on offer, be it sweet potatoes or butternut squash. I think this goes particularly well with the Chermoula Cauliflower (page 88). This is traditionally served with *chapos*, an East African flatbread, similar to an Indian chapati (page 288), but I think any bread works well.

Plantain Mash
matoke

4 plantains, each about 180g,
    ends cut off
120g butter, diced
1 teaspoon cumin seeds
1 onion, chopped
8 garlic cloves, chopped
2 long, thin green chillies,
    chopped
2 tablespoons tomato purée
1 can (400g) chopped tomatoes
a pinch of ground cinnamon
salt and ground black pepper
chopped coriander leaves,
    to garnish

Put the plantains in a saucepan of boiling water and boil over a medium-high heat for 25–30 minutes until they are tender. Drain well, peel and remove any black membrane, then mash with a potato masher, or use a grater. It's important to mash the plantains while they are still hot. Set aside.

Melt about 30g butter in a saucepan over a medium heat. Add the cumin seeds and stir until they turn darker. Add the onion and fry, stirring occasionally, until the onion softens. Add the garlic and chilli and continue stirring until the onion is lightly coloured. Don't take your eyes off the pan at this point, because the butter can easily burn. Stir the tomato purée into the onions for 1 minute to cook out the rawness. Add the canned tomatoes with a pinch of black pepper and salt to taste and give everything a good stir.

Stir in the mashed plantain, the cinnamon and the remaining butter, stirring as the butter melts so it gets incorporated. Scrape the bottom of the pan if the plantain mixture begins to catch – you want to capture any caramelisation, but you don't want any burnt flavour. Taste and adjust the salt, if necessary. Garnish with the coriander leaves and serve.

Not for the faint-hearted! This recipe contains hot chilli sauce and cayenne pepper, so you know you are in for a real chilli kick. This recipe was given to me by a friend and I have thoroughly enjoyed it from the first time I made it. Serve this with basmati rice (page 283), or for a touch of fusion, toss it with boiled spaghetti or tagliatelle.

Peanut Stew
dovi

1½ tablespoons sunflower oil
4 garlic cloves, chopped
1 large onion, chopped
350ml vegetable stock, ideally
   home-made (page 282)
350ml water plus extra,
   if needed
150g chunky or smooth
   peanut butter
3 tablespoons bottled hot
   chilli sauce
125ml passata
1 carrot, peeled and diced
1 teaspoon cayenne pepper
6 okra pods, stem ends removed
   and the pods chopped
80g spinach leaves, rinsed
sea salt

Heat the oil in a saucepan over a medium-high heat. Add the garlic and onion and fry, stirring often, until the onion is translucent. Add the vegetable stock, water, peanut butter and chilli sauce, and continue stirring until the peanut butter is incorporated. This is the base for the stew. Don't take your eyes off it, because it can thicken quite quickly.

Stir in the passata, carrot and cayenne pepper, and bring to the boil. Reduce the heat to low and leave the mixture to simmer for 8 minutes, stirring occasionally, or until the flavours blend and the carrot is becoming tender.

Add the okra and salt to taste and continue simmering over a low heat for 15 minutes, stirring often to prevent the mixture from sticking to the bottom of the pan. Cook until the okra are carrot are tender. Add a splash of water if the stew needs thinning a little. Stir in the spinach and as soon as it wilts the stew is ready to serve. Taste and adjust the salt, if necessary.

Serves 4

This family-style recipe is traditionally made with fresh sweetcorn cobs, but I've streamlined the method by using frozen kernels, straight from the freezer. For variety, stir in several handfuls of chopped kale or baby spinach leaves just before the potatoes finish cooking and continue simmering until the greens are tender. The green chilli and curry powder give this quite a kick, so serve with plenty of plain basmati rice (page 283) to balance the robust flavours.

Potato & Sweetcorn Curry
makai paka

150g frozen sweetcorn kernels
2 tablespoons sunflower oil
3 garlic cloves, finely chopped
1 green chilli, chopped
1 onion, finely chopped
4 teaspoons East African Curry Powder (page 273)
3 floury potatoes, such as King Edwards, peeled and cut into bite-sized cubes
1 can (400g) chopped tomatoes
1cm piece of fresh ginger, peeled and finely chopped
1 tablespoon freshly squeezed lemon juice, or to taste
2 tablespoons chopped coriander leaves, plus extra to garnish
250ml coconut milk
sea salt

Put the sweetcorn kernels in a dry frying pan over a high heat and fry, stirring occasionally, until they thaw, are lightly coloured and begin to pop. Any liquid that comes from the kernels will evaporate. Watch closely so none of the kernels burn. Set aside.

Heat the oil in a saucepan over a medium-high heat. Add the garlic, chilli and onion, and fry, stirring often, until the onion is lightly coloured. Add the curry powder and stir for 30 seconds to cook the ground spices. You really have to watch the pan at this point to make sure nothing catches and burns.

Stir in the potatoes, tomatoes and ginger with salt to taste. Pour in enough water to cover the potatoes and bring to the boil. Reduce the heat and leave to simmer for 15 minutes, or until the potatoes are almost tender.

When the potatoes are tender enough to be easily pierced with the tip of a knife, add the lemon juice and chopped coriander. Stir in the coconut milk and continue simmering for a few minutes for the flavours to blend, and until the potatoes are completely cooked. Adjust the lemon juice and salt, if necessary. Sprinkle with a few coriander leaves and it's ready to serve.

Left: Potato &
Sweetcorn Curry
(page 121)
Right: Peanut
Stew (page 120)

Serves 4

This is my vegetarian version of what many consider to be South Africa's national dish – with a good amount of heat from the South African curry powder. Originally from Durban, culinary legend maintains this recipe grew out of the need for cheap food during the Great Depression. South Africans and Chinese labourers quickly realised vegetarian curries from the large Indian community were one of their best options. Indians were known as 'banias' at the time and the name of Chinese stir-fries always had 'chow' at the end, so this dish was first known as Bania Chow, which eventually morphed into Bunny Chow. What's most unusual about this recipe is that it is traditionally served in a hollowed-out loaf of bread, a portable, edible container.

Bunny Chow

200g dried red kidney beans, rinsed and soaked overnight in cold water to cover
1 green chilli, split lengthwise, but left whole
2.5cm piece of fresh ginger, peeled but left whole
200g dried split brown chickpeas (*channa daal* or Bengal gram), rinsed and soaked in cold water to cover for 20 minutes
75g dried soya mince, or 250g rehydrated soya mince
3 tablespoons sunflower oil
2.5cm piece of cinnamon bark
2 green cardamom pods, bruised
1 bay leaf
1 star anise
½ teaspoon cumin seeds
½ teaspoon fennel seeds
1 onion, finely chopped
1 garlic clove, finely chopped
1 tablespoon South African Curry Powder (page 273)

First, cook the pulses (see Atul's tip, right). Drain the kidney beans, then put them in large saucepan with double their depth of salted fresh water and bring to the boil. Boil hard for 10 minutes, then skim the surface. Add the green chilli and ginger, reduce the heat to low, partially cover and simmer for 50 minutes, or until tender.

Meanwhile, drain the split chickpeas, then transfer them to another pan and add water to cover. Bring to the boil, skimming the surface, if necessary. Partially cover the pan and simmer for 20 minutes, or until tender. Drain well and set aside.

If using dried soya mince, soak the mince in freshly boiled water to cover for 15 minutes, or until tender and spongy. Drain and rinse it in running cold water, then leave it to sit in the sieve to let the excess water drain away.

Heat the oil in a large saucepan over a medium-high heat. Add the cinnamon bark, cardamom pods, bay leaf and star anise and fry, stirring, until they are aromatic. Add the cumin and fennel seeds and

2 (400g) cans chopped
  tomatoes
200ml water
2.5cm piece of fresh ginger,
  peeled and finely chopped
10–12 fresh curry leaves
2 tablespoons finely chopped
  coriander leaves
2 tablespoons freshly squeezed
  lime juice
sea salt
2 small, white unsliced loaves,
  each cut in half horizontally
  and most of the insides
  removed, to serve

continue stirring until they crackle. Add the onion
and garlic and continue stirring until the onion is
translucent.

Add the curry powder and stir for 30 seconds. Watch
closely so none of the ingredients burn. Add the soya
mince and stir for about 4 minutes until it loses its
raw appearance.

Stir in the kidney beans and chickpeas, tomatoes,
water, ginger and curry leaves with salt to taste.
Bring to the boil, then reduce the heat and leave
to simmer for about 10 minutes until the sauce
thickens and the beans are very tender.

Stir in the coriander leaves and lime juice, taste and
adjust the salt, if necessary. Spoon into the hollowed
bread halves, and it's ready to serve.

atul's tip

Anyone familiar with my style of home-cooking
knows I think nothing of starting recipes with dried
beans and lentils, because I use a pressure cooker
on an almost daily basis. My editor, however, tells
me that not everyone has one. So, if you want to
streamline this recipe use canned kidney beans
and chickpeas instead. Or, add variety with canned
cannellini beans, broad beans or green lentils. You
need a total drained weight of 400g pulses.

A friend from Johannesburg introduced me to this savoury pie on my first visit to South Africa, and it's been a part of my domestic repertoire ever since. Everyone always wants seconds, and it's good to make ahead for last-minute cooking. Complete the meal with turmeric-coloured rice and freshly boiled vegetables, such as carrots, green beans or peas.

Bobotie

150g dried soya mince, or 500g rehydrated soya mince
4 tablespoons sunflower oil
2.5cm piece of cinnamon bark
10 black peppercorns
4 green cardamom pods, bruised
3 cloves
2 dried bay leaves
1 star anise
2 onions, finely chopped
1 tablespoon South African Curry Powder (page 273)
½ teaspoon ground turmeric
100g sultanas or raisins, soaked in hot water to swell
3–4 fresh or freeze-dried Makrut lime leaves, fine central ribs removed
2 tomatoes, finely chopped
1 large apple, peeled and grated
2 tablespoons apricot jam or mango chutney
1 tablespoon freshly grated lemon or lime zest
1 teaspoon light brown sugar
1 egg, beaten
2 thick slices of bread, crumbled and soaked in 320ml whole milk
100g flaked almonds
sea salt

If using dried soya mince, soak the mince in freshly boiled water to cover for 15 minutes, or until tender and spongy. Drain and rinse in running cold water, then leave it to sit in the sieve to let the excess water drain away.

Preheat the oven to 180°C/Fan 160°C/Gas 4.

Heat the oil in a frying pan over a medium heat. Add the cinnamon bark, peppercorns, cardamom pods, cloves, bay leaves and star anise, and fry, stirring often, until they are aromatic and the seeds begin to crackle. Add the onions and continue stirring until they are lightly coloured. Add the curry powder and turmeric and stir for 30 seconds to cook the ground spices. Watch closely so nothing burns.

Add the soya mince with a good pinch of salt and stir for about 4 minutes until it loses its raw appearance. Add the sultanas, Makrut lime leaves, tomatoes, apple, apricot jam, lemon zest and brown sugar, and continue stirring for 3–5 minutes until the tomatoes start to soften.

Remove the pan from the heat and stir in the egg and soaked bread with any extra milk, breaking it up with a fork, and mix well. Add salt to taste.

Spoon the mixture into a large ovenproof serving dish and sprinkle the almonds over the top. Put on a baking sheet and bake for 30 minutes.

For the custard topping
1 egg
150ml whole milk
¼ teaspoon ground turmeric
freshly grated nutmeg, to taste

Meanwhile, whisk together all the ingredients for the custard topping.

After the soya mince mixture has baked for 30 minutes, pour over the custard. Return the dish to the oven and bake for a further 15–20 minutes until the topping is set and lightly browned.

It's ready to serve as soon as it comes out of the oven.

sub

indian
ontinent

This was my favourite childhood snack, and I still absolutely adore eating it – it's a great summertime treat in my household. My father used to add a little chopped fresh ginger, but my daughter hates ginger at the moment, so I haven't included it. Feel free to add some, if you'd like.

Chickpea Salad
channa chaat

2 floury potatoes, such as King Edwards, peeled and halved

2 x 400g cans chickpeas, drained and rinsed

2 tomatoes, finely chopped

4 tablespoons finely chopped coriander leaves

1 long, thin green chilli, finely sliced

1 red onion, finely chopped

4 tablespoons tamarind extract (see Atul's tip, page 167), or to taste

1½ teaspoons ground toasted cumin seeds (page 270)

½ teaspoon red chilli powder

¼ teaspoon black salt, or use ordinary sea salt

sea salt

Put the potatoes in a large saucepan of salted water over a high heat. Bring to the boil and boil for 20 minutes or until tender. Drain, rinse under cold running water and drain well again. Dice the potatoes and leave to cool completely.

Put the chickpeas in a large bowl. Add the potatoes, half of the tomatoes and coriander leaves, along with the green chilli, red onion, tamarind extract, ground cumin seeds, chilli powder, black salt and ordinary sea salt to taste, and stir together until all the ingredients are well mixed.

Stir in the remaining tomatoes and coriander leaves. Taste and adjust the salt and tamarind, if necessary.

I have written this recipe from memory. My mother used to cook this simple dish while I was growing up, primarily in the winter in an iron wok over a charcoal fire. The aromas were simply mesmerising – the frying of the spices and garlic are embedded in my memory. I become very nostalgic whenever I cook this recipe. You could add a dried red chilli for extra heat if you wish.

Punjabi Fenugreek Potatoes
methi aloo

4 tablespoons mustard oil (I use a blend of mustard oil and rapeseed oil available in supermarkets)
1 teaspoon cumin seeds
2 large garlic cloves, sliced
1 long, thin green chilli, sliced
500g new potatoes, scrubbed and quartered
1 teaspoon red chilli powder
1 teaspoon ground turmeric
500g fresh fenugreek leaves, chopped and rinsed (or use frozen and add straight from the freezer)
1 tablespoon dried fenugreek leaves
sea salt

Heat the oil in a large frying pan with a lid over a medium-high heat. Add the cumin seeds and fry, stirring, until the seeds crackle. Add the garlic and the green chilli and continue stirring to cook the garlic and flavour the oil. The heat is quite high, so keep your eye on the garlic, because it can burn quickly.

Add the potatoes and stir them around so they are coated in the spices and flavoured oil. Add the chilli powder, turmeric and salt to taste, and fry for 30 seconds, stirring, to cook the ground spices. Watch closely so they do not burn.

Add the fresh fenugreek leaves and continue stirring until the leaves wilt. Reduce the heat to medium, cover the pan and leave the potatoes to cook for 15–20 minutes, stirring occasionally, until the they are almost tender.

Uncover the pan and continue cooking for 5–10 minutes, stirring often, until the potatoes are tender. Keep an eye on the mixture and, as it catches on the bottom of the pan, use your spoon to scrape off the crusty bits and mix them in with the potatoes and leaves. I love that flavour – but you really have to watch closely so you get a caramelised flavour, not a burnt one. Crumble in the dried fenugreek leaves, taste and adjust the salt, if necessary.

Left: Paneer in Tomato & Cashew
Gravy (page 136)
Right: Chickpea Salad (page 132)
Bottom: Punjabi Fenugreek
Potatoes (page 133)

This a very rich, classic North Indian dish, popular in restaurants. I think the best way to streamline this recipe for home-cooking is to make the gravy in advance. That way when you come to finish the dish, it's all very straightforward.

Paneer in Tomato & Cashew Gravy
paneer lababdar

30g butter
1 dried bay leaf
1 onion, finely chopped
1 teaspoon ground coriander
½ teaspoon red chilli powder
½ teaspoon ground cumin
1 tablespoon tomato purée
1 teaspoon dried fenugreek leaves
1 teaspoon sugar
½ teaspoon Atul's Garam Masala (page 271)
200g paneer, cut into bite-sized cubes, plus extra, finely grated, to garnish
2 tablespoons chopped fresh coriander, plus extra to garnish
125ml single cream
sea salt

For the tomato gravy
1 can (400g) chopped tomatoes
125ml water
1.5cm piece of fresh ginger, peeled and chopped
12 unsalted raw cashew nuts
3 garlic cloves, peeled
2 green cardamom pods, bruised
2 cloves
1 teaspoon finely chopped fresh green chilli

First, make the tomato gravy. Empty the can of tomatoes into a saucepan. Add the water, ginger, cashew nuts, garlic, green cardamom pods, cloves and green chilli, and bring to the boil. Leave to simmer for 10–15 minutes until the cashews soften.

Tip the mixture into a blender or food processor and process until smooth. Set aside.

Meanwhile, melt the butter with the bay leaf in a saucepan over a medium-high heat, stirring until the butter is sizzling. Add the onion with a pinch of salt and fry, stirring often, until the onion is light brown.

Add the ground coriander, red chilli powder and ground cumin, and stir for 30 seconds to cook the spices. Stir in the tomato gravy and the tomato purée with a pinch of salt, but remember the onion has been salted. Bring to the boil, then reduce the heat and leave the gravy to simmer, uncovered, for 30 minutes, or until it is reduced to the desired consistency.

Crumble in the fenugreek leaves, rubbing them between your palms, then add the sugar and garam masala and stir everything together. Stir in the paneer and chopped coriander, then stir in the single cream. Adjust the salt, if necessary, and return to the boil. When the paneer is hot, garnish with grated paneer and chopped coriander to serve.

This is my signature dal, and one I love to cook. It's great to make ahead, so it is ideal for quick lunches or suppers. If you do cook it in advance, be sure to let it cool completely, then cover, and it will keep for up to 2 days in the fridge. Just reheat when you want to serve.

Atul's Signature Makhani Dal
mah di daal

150g dried whole black lentils (*urid dal*), rinsed and soaked overnight in cold water

50g dried red kidney beans, rinsed and soaked overnight in cold water to cover

1 long, thin green chilli, chopped

2cm piece of fresh ginger, peeled and chopped

2 tablespoons sunflower oil

1 teaspoon cumin seeds

5 garlic cloves, finely chopped

1 large onion, finely chopped

1 tablespoon ground coriander

1 teaspoon red chilli powder

1 teaspoon ground fenugreek

1 teaspoon Atul's Garam Masala (page 271)

150ml passata

1 tablespoon tomato purée

1 tablespoon lemon juice

45g butter, diced

100ml single cream

sea salt

Drain and rinse both pulses. Put them in a saucepan with a lid with double their depth of salted fresh water and bring to the boil. Boil hard for 10 minutes, then skim the surface. Add the green chilli and ginger, reduce the heat to low and simmer, partially covered, for 50 minutes, or until both pulses are very tender. Set aside without draining and they will continue to absorb liquid as they cool.

Heat the oil in a saucepan over a medium heat. Add the cumin seeds and fry, stirring, until they crackle. Add the garlic and continue stirring until it is light brown. Watch closely so it doesn't burn. Add the onion with a pinch of salt and continue frying, stirring often, until it is light brown. Stir in the ground coriander, red chilli powder, ground fenugreek and garam masala, and stir for about 30 seconds to cook the spices.

Stir in the passata and tomato purée. Reduce the heat to very low and simmer for 10 minutes, stirring often, to cook the tomato purée and blend the flavours.

Add the cooked black lentils and kidney beans with any remaining liquid and bring to the boil. Reduce the heat and leave to simmer, uncovered, for 12–15 minutes until thickened, stirring frequently so the pulses don't catch on the bottom of the pan. Stir in the lemon juice, butter and cream with salt to taste.

This dish is my personal favourite dal recipe, and when it's freshly made I think the flavours are simply amazing. It's a very Indian thing to go to street-side cafés for dal and *roti*. When this or similar dal recipes are on the menu at my restaurants, I serve them with flatbreads cooked in a tandoor oven, but at home I recommend parathas (page 289).

Street Café Dal
dhaba daal

200g split yellow peas (*toor daal* or split pigeon peas), rinsed and soaked in cold water to cover for 20 minutes
750ml water
½ teaspoon ground turmeric
3 tomatoes, chopped
sea salt
freshly squeezed lemon juice, to taste

For the tarka
1 tablespoon ghee
7.5g butter
3 garlic cloves, finely chopped
1 teaspoon cumin seeds
1 teaspoon black mustard seeds
1 large dried red chilli
8–10 fresh or dried curry leaves
2 long, thin green chillies, split lengthwise
½ teaspoon red chilli powder

To garnish
fried curry leaves
fried red chillies
chilli oil

Drain the split peas, then place them in a large saucepan with a lid over a medium-high heat with the water, turmeric and ½ teaspoon salt, and stir together. Bring to the boil, skimming the surface, if necessary, then lower the heat a little and leave to simmer for 5 minutes. Stir in the tomatoes, cover the pan and simmer for 10–15 minutes until the split peas are very tender. Use the back of a spoon to lightly crush the split peas and tomatoes against the side of the pan. Set aside and keep hot.

To make the tarka, melt the ghee and butter together in a frying pan over a medium-high heat until sizzling. Reduce the heat to medium, add the garlic and stir constantly until it just starts to brown. The aroma should be amazing at this point. Add the cumin seeds, mustard seeds and red chilli, and continue stirring until the seeds crackle and pop. Watch closely so the garlic doesn't burn.

Stir in the curry leaves, green chillies and chilli powder, then quickly add a ladleful of the lentil mixture to this pan. Tip the contents of this pan into the split peas and stir together.

Return the split peas to the boil. Stir in the lemon juice and adjust the salt, if necessary. Garnish with the fried curry leaves and red chillies, and a generous glug of chilli oil, and serve.

Try this for breakfast – I guarantee it will kickstart your day. Many Indian vegetarians don't eat eggs, so scrambled paneer has become a replacement for scrambled eggs, and another version is to replace the sweetcorn and peas with finely chopped multi-coloured peppers. I also think this makes a good late-night supper when it's essential to eat something and I'm tired, but not very hungry. In most Indian homes it is served with parathas (page 289).

Scrambled Paneer, Sweetcorn & Peas
paneer makai mutter bjurji

2 tablespoons sunflower oil
½ teaspoon cumin seeds
1 garlic clove, chopped
½ long, thin green chilli, sliced
1 teaspoon peeled and chopped
   fresh ginger
1 onion, chopped
2 teaspoons ground coriander
1 teaspoon ground turmeric
½ teaspoon red chilli powder
75g frozen sweetcorn kernels
75g frozen peas
1 tomato, chopped
50g paneer, grated
½ teaspoon mango powder
   (*amchur*) or lemon juice
1 tablespoon chopped
   coriander leaves
sea salt

Heat the oil in a large frying pan over a medium-high heat. Add the cumin seeds and fry, stirring, until they crackle. Add the garlic, green chilli and ginger, and fry, stirring, for 1 minute to flavour the oil and cook the garlic and ginger. Add the onion with a pinch of salt and continue stirring until the onion starts to become translucent. Add the ground coriander, turmeric and chilli powder, and stir for 30 seconds to cook the ground spices. Watch closely so none of the ingredients burn.

Add the sweetcorn kernels and peas and continue stirring. When the spices start sticking to the bottom of the pan, add the tomato and continue stirring, scraping up any crusty bits. Stir in the paneer with the mango powder, chopped coriander and salt to taste, and stir everything together, scraping the bottom of the pan, if necessary.

When the sweetcorn kernels and peas are thawed and hot, adjust the salt, if necessary, and serve.

One of the characteristics of Rajasthani cuisine is that there is always a great deal of work involved in the cooking. It is a rich cuisine, but it has grown out of harsh, sun-baked conditions, so cooks have always had to be inventive with their use of ingredients, thus creating labour-intensive recipes. The potatoes in this recipe are first pan-fried and then cooked with a spicy tomato-and-onion gravy. I like to serve this with millet bread and basmati rice (page 283), but, of course, any flatbread is good.

Rajasthani Onions & Potatoes
aloo pyaz ki subji

sunflower oil

4 floury potatoes, such King Edwards, peeled and each cut into 8 wedges

2 small onions or shallots, quartered

2 black cardamom pods, bruised

2 green cardamom pods, bruised

2 cloves

1 dried bay leaf

a small piece of cinnamon or cassia bark

a small piece of mace blade

1 teaspoon cumin seeds

180g Onion Paste (page 280)

1 teaspoon Ginger-Garlic Paste (page 281)

½ teaspoon Kashmiri chilli powder, or use ordinary red chilli powder

½ teaspoon sweet paprika

1 small green chilli, split lengthwise, but left whole

250ml passata

1 tablespoon ground coriander

1 teaspoon Atul's Garam Masala (page 271)

Heat a thin layer of oil in a large frying pan with a lid over a medium heat. Add as many potato wedges as will fit in a single layer, cover the pan and fry, uncovering and using tongs to turn the wedges occasionally, until they are golden brown all over. Transfer to a large plate lined with kitchen paper to drain and set aside. Add a little extra oil to the pan, if necessary, between batches.

Next repeat with the onions, uncovering the pan and turning them occasionally, until they are caramelised. Transfer to the plate and set aside.

Meanwhile, heat 4 tablespoons oil in another large frying pan over a medium-high heat. Add the black and green cardamom pods, cloves, bay leaf, cinnamon and mace, and stir together. Add the cumin seeds and continue stirring until the seeds crackle.

Reduce the heat to low, add the onion paste and fry, stirring, until the paste and flavourings are combined. Stir in the ginger-garlic paste and fry, stirring frequently, for 1 minute to cook the ginger. Increase the heat to medium, add the chilli powder, paprika and green chilli, and continue stirring

¼ teaspoon black salt, or use
  extra ordinary sea salt
125g full-fat natural yogurt
125ml single cream
1 tablespoon dried fenugreek
  leaves
500ml water
2 spring onions, finely chopped
sea salt
chopped coriander leaves,
  to garnish

to cook the ground spices. Add the passata and continue stirring for 3–5 minutes so the tomato is well cooked and won't taste acidic in the final dish.

Add the ground coriander, garam masala, black salt, if using, and sea salt to taste, and stir for 30 seconds. It should be smelling really fantastic at this point. Whisk the yogurt until very smooth, then add it to the pan and stir to blend into the tomato sauce. Now stir in the cream, then crumble the fenugreek leaves between your palms into the pan and continue stirring.

Stir in the water and spring onions, then leave the gravy to simmer, uncovered, for 15 minutes. Add the potatoes and continue simmering until the potatoes are very tender and the tip of a knife slides in easily. Just before serving, stir in the onions and keep simmering until they are hot. Taste and adjust the salt, if necessary. Sprinkle with coriander leaves and serve.

● atul's tip

If you want to make this more substantial, add 200g paneer, cut into bite-sized cubes. Pan-fry the cubes before you fry the potatoes until they are lightly coloured, then set aside. Add them to the simmering gravy with the potatoes.

Ground fennel seeds and black pepper are often used in Kashmiri cooking, and for major impact I recommend you grind your own fennel seeds, rather than using ground fennel (page 270). In my restaurants the paneer for this dish would be deep-fried, but I don't want to do that at home, so I suggest pan-frying it instead.

Kashmiri Paneer in Spicy Milk Gravy
chaman kaliya

sunflower oil
200g paneer, cut into bite-sized cubes, plus a little extra, finely grated, to garnish
15g butter
3 green cardamom pods, bruised
2 cloves
1 small dried bay leaf
1 teaspoon cumin seeds
a small piece of cinnamon bark
1 teaspoon Kashmiri red chilli powder, or use ordinary red chilli powder
1 teaspoon ground coriander
1 teaspoon ground fennel seeds (page 270)
½ teaspoon ground black pepper
½ teaspoon ground turmeric
250ml semi-skimmed milk
¼ teaspoon sugar
a small pinch of saffron powder
1 tablespoon dried fenugreek leaves, or 1 teaspoon ground fenugreek seeds
sea salt
chopped coriander leaves, to garnish

First, make the spiced onion paste. Put the onions in a heavy-based saucepan with water to cover. Cover the pan and bring to the boil, then simmer for 8–10 minutes until a knife slides into the onions easily. This process removes the bitterness from the onions. Drain well, then roughly chop and pat dry.

Transfer the onions, along with the garlic, water and ginger to a food processor, and process until a fine paste forms. Set aside.

Heat a thin layer of sunflower oil in a non-stick frying pan with a lid over a medium heat. Add the paneer, spread it out in a single layer, cover the pan and fry, uncovering and turning occasionally using tongs, until it's lightly browned all over. This will take about 10 minutes. I think a bit of colour is desirable in a dish like this.

Meanwhile, melt the butter with 2 tablespoons oil in another large frying pan over a medium-high heat. Add the cardamom pods, cloves, bay leaf, cumin seeds and cinnamon bark, stirring until the seeds crackle and start to brown. Stir in the spiced onion paste and fry, stirring, for 1 minute to cook the rawness out of the garlic and ginger before adding the ground spices.

Add the Kashmiri chilli powder, ground coriander, ground fennel seeds, black pepper, turmeric and salt to taste, and stir for about 5 minutes until the spiced

For the spiced onion paste

2 onions, halved

3 garlic cloves, peeled and
  coarsely chopped

4 tablespoons water

2.5cm piece of fresh ginger,
  peeled and finely chopped

onion paste turns light brown and becomes drier looking. Watch closely so nothing catches on the bottom of the pan and burns. And, don't forget to keep an eye on the paneer so it colours all over, but doesn't burn.

Reduce the heat under the pan with the spiced onion paste and stir in the milk, sugar and saffron powder. Crumble the fenugreek leaves between your palms into the pan.

Add the paneer to the gravy and stir it in. Taste and adjust the salt, if necessary. Garnish with coriander and grated paneer and serve.

Makes 16 koftas

This is one of the few complex recipes in the book, but it's good for celebrations. You can prepare a lot of it in advance; the koftas will keep covered in the fridge for 24 hours and the gravy can be made in advance and reheated, adding extra water if needed. It's important to thoroughly crush the peas; they are essential to help bind the kofta mixture, so use a potato masher.

Kofta Curry
shahi kofta curry

sunflower oil
a large pinch of asafoetida
½ teaspoon cumin seeds
1cm piece of fresh ginger,
    peeled and finely chopped
1 green chilli, finely chopped
1 garlic clove, finely chopped
200g floury potatoes, such as
    King Edwards, peeled and
    grated
140g carrot, peeled and grated
80g cauliflower florets, grated
200g frozen peas, thawed,
    patted dry and crushed
100g cored, deseeded and
    finely chopped *mixed* yellow
    and green peppers, about
    ½ pepper each
1 teaspoon ground coriander
½ teaspoon red chilli powder
½ teaspoon ground turmeric
a large pinch of Atul's Garam
    Masala (page 271)
a large pinch of dried fenugreek
    leaves
90g paneer, finely grated
2 tablespoons melon seeds
2 tablespoons sultanas, chopped
4 tablespoons chickpea flour
    (*besan*)

Heat 3 tablespoons of oil in a large wok or frying pan over a medium-high heat. Add the asafoetida and stir until it foams and subsides. Add the cumin seeds and fry until they crackle. Add the ginger, green chilli and garlic, and stir for 1 minute. Add the potatoes and keep stirring; they can easily catch on the bottom of the pan, so it's important all the pieces get well coated with the oil. Stir in the carrot and cauliflower, then add the peas and peppers and stir until everything is mixed together.

Add the ground coriander, chilli powder, turmeric, garam masala and salt to taste. Crumble in the fenugreek leaves, then stir for 30 seconds. Stir in the paneer, melon seeds and sultanas. Use a wooden spoon to scrape any caramelised bits off the bottom of the pan – you want to include them. Set aside.

Meanwhile, put the chickpea flour in a dry frying pan over a medium-high heat and toast, stirring constantly, until it turns light brown. Immediately remove the pan from the heat, and keep stirring to prevent the flour overcooking.

Stir 2 tablespoons of the toasted chickpea flour into the vegetable mixture, reserving the rest, then add the breadcrumbs; the mixture should be soft, but not wet. It shouldn't stick to your fingers. Taste and adjust the salt, if necessary. Form the mixture into 16 balls, each about the size of a lime. Set aside.

30g fine fresh wholemeal
   breadcrumbs
sunflower oil
60g unsalted cashew nuts,
   soaked in hot water to cover
   for 30–40 minutes
sea salt
single cream, to garnish
pea shoots or chopped
   coriander leaves, to garnish

For the gravy

60g unsalted cashew nuts,
   soaked in hot water to cover
   for 30–40 minutes
2 tablespoons sunflower oil
2 small dried bay leaves
2 green cardamom pods, bruised
1 black cardamom pod, bruised
a small blade of cinnamon bark
a small blade of mace
240g Onion Paste (page 280)
1½ teaspoons Ginger-Garlic
   Paste (page 281)
250ml passata
½ teaspoon Atul's Garam Masala
   (page 271)
¼ teaspoon red chilli powder
¼ teaspoon ground turmeric
4 tablespoons full-fat natural
   yogurt, whisked
250ml water
2 tablespoons single cream
a large pinch of dried fenugreek
   leaves

To make the gravy, drain the cashew nuts, reserving 4 tablespoons of the water. Put the nuts and the reserved water in a food processor and process until a thin, smooth paste forms. Set aside.

Heat the 2 tablespoons sunflower oil in a large frying pan over a medium-high heat. Add the bay leaves, cardamom pods, cinnamon and mace, and stir to flavour the oil. Add the onion and ginger-garlic pastes and stir for 1 minute. Stir in the passata and simmer for 3–5 minutes. Stir in ¼ teaspoon of the garam masala, the chilli powder and turmeric, and stir for 30 seconds to cook the ground spices.

Stir the cashew nut paste, then add it to the gravy. Add the yogurt and reduce the heat. Keep stirring over a low heat until the mixture is combined and thickened. Stir in the water and leave the gravy to simmer while you fry the koftas, stirring the sauce occasionally.

Heat enough oil for deep-frying to 180°C in a deep-fat fryer or heavy-based saucepan. Line a baking tray or large plate with kitchen paper.

Roll the vegetable koftas in the reserved chickpea flour, gently changing the shape from round to oval. Make them nice and compact so no pieces of vegetables fall out while they are frying.

Add as many koftas that will fit in the pan without overcrowding and deep-fry until they are golden brown all over, which only takes about 30 seconds. The vegetables are already cooked so you are only sealing the koftas and heating them through. As they are fried, use a slotted spoon to transfer to the paper-lined tray and keep hot while you fry the rest. Be sure to reheat the oil to the correct temperature between batches.

Just before serving, strain the gravy into another pan. Stir the cream, then crumble in the fenugreek leaves and add the remaining ¼ teaspoon garam masala. Bring to a boil, stirring. Taste and adjust the seasoning, if necessary, garnish and serve.

Serves 4

One distinctive feature of biryanis from the Kolkata region is that they contain potatoes. Culinary legend says this came about after the Nawab of Awadh was exiled in 1865 from Lucknow to a suburb of modern-day Kolkata. As a man who loved the rich Mughal food of the north, he took many cooks with him, but as they all eventually left his employment he had to rely on local cooks, who cooked extensively with potatoes. Using ghee for richness, rather than the more typical vegetable oil or coconut oil of the region, is another legacy from the Mughal kitchens.

Kolkata Vegetable Biryani
kolkata torkari pulao

1½ tablespoons ghee, plus 1 teaspoon extra for the saffron milk

2 tablespoons sunflower oil

1 dried bay leaf

1 onion, thinly sliced

2 potatoes, such as King Edwards, peeled and cut into bite-sized pieces

1 carrot, peeled and cut into 1cm cubes

150g fresh or frozen peas

75g cauliflower florets

2 teaspoons Ginger-Garlic Paste (page 281)

2 teaspoons Atul's Garam Masala (page 271)

1 teaspoon red chilli powder

1 teaspoon ground coriander

½ teaspoon ground turmeric

250g full-fat natural yogurt, whisked

250ml water

4 tablespoons whole milk

a pinch of saffron threads

2 tablespoons single cream

First, cook the rice. Bring a saucepan of water to the boil. Drain the rice and add it to the boiling water with the cardamom pods, bay leaves, cinnamon, salt, and ghee, and simmer for 8 minutes, or until it is just al dente. You do not want it completely tender at this point. Drain well and set aside until required.

Meanwhile, melt the 1½ tablespoons of ghee with the oil in a large frying pan with a lid over a medium-high heat. Add the bay leaf and onion and fry, stirring often, for 8–10 minutes until the onion is dark golden brown. Transfer about half the onion slices to a plate lined with kitchen paper and set aside to drain. Use the spoon to press the slices against the side of the pan as you are taking them out to remove as much oil as possible. These will be layered in biryani and add hugely to the flavour.

Stir the potatoes and carrot into the onion remaining in the pan, followed by the peas and cauliflower florets with salt to taste. Add the ginger-garlic paste and continue stirring for 1 minute to cook out the raw flavour. Add the garam masala, chilli powder, ground coriander and turmeric, and stir for 30 seconds to cook the ground spices. Watch closely so nothing burns.

a large handful of mint or
  coriander leaves, finely
  chopped
rosewater
sea salt
Mint Raita (page 292), to serve

For the rice
200g white basmati rice, rinsed
  under cold water until the
  water runs clear, then left
  to soak in a bowl of water
  for 30 minutes
4 black cardamom pods, bruised
2 dried bay leaves
2.5cm piece of cinnamon bark
1½ teaspoons salt
1 teaspoon ghee

Stir in the yogurt and water, using the spoon to
scrape up any browned bits from the bottom of
the pan. Cover the pan, lower the heat and leave to
simmer for about 15 minutes, stirring occasionally,
until all the vegetables are tender. Taste and adjust
the salt, if necessary.

Meanwhile, preheat the oven to 200°C/Fan 180°C/
Gas 6. Put the milk and saffron in a small pan over
a low heat and leave to infuse. Just before you start
to assemble the dish, add the cream and an extra
1 teaspoon ghee to the saffron milk, stirring until
the ghee melts.

To assemble the biryani, spoon a layer of half the
vegetables into an ovenproof casserole that is
suitable for serving from. Cover the base completely
with a layer of rice, then sprinkle with mint, add
about half of the reserved onions and drizzle with
the saffron milk. Add a few splashes of rosewater.
Repeat the layering, being sure to include all the
vegetable cooking juices.

Cover the casserole and put it on a baking tray. Cook
in the oven for 15 minutes, or until piping hot. It's
ready to serve with raita on the side.

This is a favourite recipe, and it is often on the menu in my restaurants. My father was an absolute pro at making this, and it also featured quite a bit during my time working in East India. It's a popular recipe for large family celebrations, because it is particularly good when made a day in advance and reheated.

Bengali Yellow Peas
ghugni

400g dry whole yellow peas, rinsed and soaked overnight in water to cover
2 dried bay leaves
1 black cardamom pod, bruised
a small piece of cinnamon bark
2½ tablespoons sunflower oil
1 teaspoon cumin seeds
1 onion, chopped
2 green cardamom pods, bruised
1 tomato, chopped
¼ teaspoon red chilli powder
½ teaspoon ground turmeric
2–3 tablespoons water
1.5cm piece of fresh ginger, peeled and finely chopped
½ long, thin green chilli
5cm piece of fresh coconut, peeled and cut into very thin pieces, or use frozen grated coconut
2 teaspoons ground toasted cumin seeds (page 270)
1 tablespoon tamarind extract (see Atul's tip, page 167)
½ teaspoon Atul's Garam Masala (page 271)
sea salt

Drain the yellow peas, then put them in a large saucepan with a lid with fresh water to cover and bring to the boil, skimming the surface as necessary. Boil hard for 10 minutes, then skim the surface. Reduce the heat, add 1 bay leaf, the cardamom pod and cinnamon bark, cover and leave to simmer for 50 minutes–1 hour until the peas are tender. Add salt to taste. Drain and remove the whole spices – they have done their job. Reserve the cooking liquid and set it and the peas aside.

Heat the oil in a large frying pan over a medium-high heat. Add the remaining bay leaf and cumin seeds and fry, stirring, until the seeds crackle. Add the onion with a pinch of salt and continue stirring until it is translucent. Add the green cardamom pods and stir until the onion turns light brown, watching so it doesn't burn.

Stir in the tomato, then add the chilli powder and turmeric and stir for 30 seconds to cook the ground spices. Add the water to help the tomatoes soften. Stir in the ginger and green chilli and continue stirring until the water evaporates.

When the tomatoes have softened, add the yellow peas, enough of the reserved cooking liquid to just cover the beans, the coconut pieces, ground cumin seeds, tamarind extract and garam masala. Stir and bring to the boil. Taste and adjust the salt, if necessary, and it's ready to serve.

Slightly sweet, this dal is often served at celebrations. I'm always tempted to add a little green chilli to this, but I have resisted, because it is not traditional. Whatever little heat do you get in this dish comes from the ginger, and the flavour from the cinnamon, cardamom, coconut and ginger is just beautiful.

Bengali Dal
cholar daal

200g dried split brown chickpeas (*channa daal* or Bengal gram), rinsed and soaked in cold water to cover for 20 minutes
1 dried bay leaf
¼ teaspoon ground turmeric
1 tablespoon ghee
½ tablespoon sunflower oil
2 green cardamom pods, bruised
2 cloves
2.5cm piece of cinnamon bark
1 teaspoon black mustard seeds
50g fresh or frozen grated coconut, or use chopped coconut chips
2 tablespoons sultanas
1cm piece of fresh ginger, peeled and chopped
125ml coconut milk
1 tablespoon grated jaggery or Demerara sugar
sea salt
chopped coriander leaves, to garnish

Drain the split brown chickpeas, then transfer them to a saucepan with a lid with fresh water to cover, the bay leaf, turmeric, and salt to taste, and bring to the boil, skimming the surface if necessary. Partially cover the pan and simmer for 20 minutes or until tender. Set aside without draining.

Melt the ghee with the oil in a large frying pan or wok over a medium-high heat. Add the cardamom pods, cloves, cinnamon and mustard seeds, and fry, stirring, until the mustard seeds pop. Add the coconut, sultanas and ginger, and stir constantly for 1 minute to cook the ginger. Watch closely.

When the coconut becomes light brown, pour in the cooked split chickpeas with their cooking liquid and add salt to taste, but remember the cooking water has been salted. Bring to the boil, stirring and mashing some of the split chickpeas with the back of your spoon. Leave to boil for a few minutes, then stir in the coconut milk and jaggery and continue simmering, uncovered, 5–10 minutes until the mixture thickens to a consistency you like. Taste and adjust the salt, if necessary. Garnish with coriander and serve.

Bottle gourds are a type of squash popular throughout Asia, but not always easily available elsewhere. If you can't find them, this spicy-hot recipe is equally successful made with courgettes. Mong dal nuggets are made of lentils that are sun-dried. They can also be made with other lentils such as urid dal, and I've also seen them called lentil kisses.

Bottle Gourd Curry
lauki curry

2 tablespoons sunflower oil

100g sun-dried mong dal nuggets (*moong wadi*), broken into pieces

2 tablespoons mustard oil (I use a blend of mustard oil and rapeseed oil available in supermarkets)

5cm piece of cinnamon bark

2 dried bay leaves

2 cloves

1 long, thin green chilli, finely chopped

2 teaspoons cumin seeds

3cm piece of fresh ginger, peeled and chopped

500g bottle gourd or courgette, peeled and thinly sliced

2 teaspoons ground coriander

1 teaspoon red chilli powder

1 teaspoon ground cumin

1 teaspoon ground turmeric

2 tomatoes, chopped

1 lemon, halved

sea salt

chopped fresh coriander, to garnish

Heat the oil in a large frying pan over a medium-high heat. Add the dal nugget pieces and fry, stirring, to make them crisper. Tip them on to a plate and leave to cool, then put three-quarters of them in a spice grinder, coffee grinder or food processor and grind or process until a coarse powder forms. Set the powder and un-ground nuggets aside.

Heat the mustard oil in a saucepan with a lid over a medium-high heat. Add the cinnamon, bay leaves and cloves, and fry, stirring, until the spices sizzle. Add the green chilli and cumin seeds and stir until the seeds crackle. Add the ginger and stir constantly until it starts to colour, but watch closely so it doesn't burn.

Stir in the bottle gourd. Add the ground coriander, red chilli powder, ground cumin, turmeric and salt to taste, and stir for 30 seconds to cook the spices. Add the tomatoes and the ground dal nuggets and stir together. Cover, lower the heat and leave to cook gently in the condensation that gathers in the pan until the gourd is tender. Taste and adjust the salt if necessary.

Sprinkle with the reserved dal nuggets for a bit of crunch, squeeze over 2 tablespoons lemon juice and stir together. Sprinkle with the coriander and serve.

Serves 4–6

My grandfather had four jackfruit trees in his garden in Jamshedpur, in eastern India, where every house used to have jackfruit trees, and the thick leaves were used to make disposable plates for the street hawkers. Consequently, this tree was always around me during my childhood. I hated eating the jackfruit as a child, but have grown up to love it. In its ripe form, it's eaten raw, but here I'm treating it as a cooked vegetable.

Jackfruit & Pepper Stir-fry
kali mirch ka kathal

4 x 400g cans jackfruit pieces, drained and patted dry
3 tablespoons coconut oil
3 tablespoons rapeseed oil
15–18 fresh curry leaves, plus a few extra to garnish
2 green chillies, chopped
2 garlic cloves, chopped
2 onions, thinly sliced
1 green pepper, cored, deseeded and thinly sliced
3cm piece of fresh ginger, peeled and chopped
¼ teaspoon Kashmiri chilli powder, or to taste
2 teaspoons ground coriander
½ teaspoon garam masala
1 tablespoon ground fennel seeds (page 270)
½ teaspoon ground black pepper, or to taste
2 tablespoons cider vinegar
sea salt

For the curry paste
2 tablespoons rapeseed oil
1 tablespoon ground coriander
2 teaspoons ground turmeric
1½ teaspoons cornflour

Mix all the ingredients for the curry paste together in a large bowl. Add the jackfruit pieces and stir around until they are well coated.

Heat a large frying pan over a high heat. Add the spiced jackfruit and fry, stirring, for 4–5 minutes until the pieces are caramelised all over. Cook in batches, if necessary. Remove from the pan and set aside.

Heat a large wok over a high heat. Add the coconut and rapeseed oils and swirl them around. Add the curry leaves, green chillies, garlic, onions, green pepper, ginger and salt to taste, and stir-fry until the onions are light brown.

Add the fried jackfruit followed by the chilli powder, ground coriander, garam masala, ground fennel and black pepper, and continue stir-frying for 2–3 minutes to mix all the ingredients and until the green pepper is tender. Keep your eyes on the wok so nothing burns.

Add the vinegar and toss the mixture well. Taste and adjust the salt, if necessary. Garnish with the extra curry leaves and serve.

The recipe comes from the Indian state of Odisha, where it is made in vast quantities to feed Hindus on pilgrimage to the local temples. *Panch phoron* is particular to Bengal, made up of equal quantities of cumin seeds, fennel seeds, fenugreek seeds, onion seeds and *radhuni*, a typical Bengali spice.

Lentil & Vegetable Stew
dalma

50g split yellow peas (*toor daal* or split pigeon peas)
50g split yellow mung dal (*moong daal*)
150g shelled peas
1 small carrot, peeled and thinly sliced
1 small potato, peeled, halved and thinly sliced
1 small sweet potato, peeled, halved and thinly sliced
a handful of green beans, topped, tailed and chopped
2.5cm piece of fresh ginger, peeled
1 teaspoon ground turmeric
sea salt

For the tarka
1½ tablespoons sunflower oil
¼ teaspoon asafoetida
1 dried bay leaf
1 dried red chilli
1 teaspoon cumin seeds
1 teaspoon *panch phoron*

To garnish
red chilli powder or hot paprika
fresh or frozen grated coconut
chopped coriander leaves

Rinse both the split yellow peas and split yellow mung dal and soak individually in enough cold water to cover for 20 minutes.

Drain the pulses, then transfer to a large saucepan with a lid with plenty of water and a pinch of salt. Bring to the boil over a high heat, skimming the surface, if necessary, then cover and simmer for 15 minutes, or until both are tender.

Stir in the peas, carrot, potato, sweet potato and green beans. Grate the ginger directly into the pan, then add the turmeric. Stir in enough cold water to cover the vegetables, if necessary. Cover the pan and bring to the boil. Reduce the heat and leave to gently bubble for 7 minutes, or until the vegetables are tender. Use the back of a large spoon to mash some of the pulses and vegetables against the side of the pan to thicken the stew.

Just before serving, make the tarka. Heat the oil in a small frying pan over a high heat. Add the asafoetida and stir until it foams and subsides. Add the bay leaf, red chilli, cumin seeds and *panch phoron*, and stir until the seeds crackle and pop. Immediately pour into the stew – be careful because it will sputter. If you have any seeds left in the small pan, add a little of the lentil mixture and stir around to 'deglaze' the pan. Bring to the boil, taste and adjust the salt, if necessary. Garnish and it's ready to serve.

*Serves 4
as a sharing
dish*

This is a delicious straightforward, quick recipe from Andhra Pradesh that is perfect served with freshly boiled basmati rice (page 283) or flatbread. I also recommend it served family-style with Kolkata Vegetable Biryani (page 150) or Jackfruit & Pepper Stir-fry (page 158) and Omani Flatbread (page 258).

Tomato Curry
tamater pachadi

20g unsalted skinned peanuts
2 tablespoons coconut oil or
  sunflower oil
¼ teaspoon asafoetida
1 long, thin green chilli, sliced
  lengthwise
½ teaspoon cumin seeds
½ teaspoon black mustard seeds
1 onion, chopped
3 large tomatoes, chopped
6–8 fresh or dried curry leaves
½ teaspoon ground turmeric
¼ teaspoon red chilli powder
125ml coconut milk
sea salt

Ground peanuts are used to thicken this dish, but they have to be toasted first. Heat a dry frying pan over a medium-high heat, add the peanuts and stir for about 1 minute until lightly browned. Immediately tip them out of the pan and leave to cool. Transfer to a spice grinder or coffee grinder, or use a pestle and mortar, and grind until finely ground. Set aside.

Melt the coconut oil in a saucepan with a lid over a medium-high heat. Add the asafoetida and stir until foams and subsides. Add the green chilli, cumin seeds and mustard seeds, and stir until they crackle and pop. Add the onion with a pinch of salt and fry, stirring often, until the onion becomes translucent.

Add the tomatoes and curry leaves and stir them into the onion and spices. Lower the heat, cover the pan and leave to cook until the tomato skins start shrivelling.

Increase the heat to medium-high. Add the turmeric and chilli powder with a pinch of salt to taste, and stir for 30 seconds to cook the ground spices. Add the ground peanuts and stir everything together. Stir in the coconut milk and leave to simmer, uncovered, until the mixture thickens to a texture you like. Taste and adjust the salt, if necessary.

You might not think of making a curry with cucumbers, but believe me it works. I first encountered this style of curry from Tamil Nadu when I was a young trainee chef. Cashew nuts, which grow in abundance in the region, give a real richness to this curry. Serve this with basmati rice (page 283), dosas (rice pancakes) or even hoppers (page 286) from Sri Lanka.

Cashew & Cucumber Curry
kazambu

200g unsalted cashew nuts, soaked in water to cover for 30–40 minutes
2 tablespoons coconut oil
1–2 dried cascabel chillies, to taste (see Atul's tip, below)
½ teaspoon black mustard seeds
¼ teaspoon cumin seeds
10 fresh or dried curry leaves
1 onion, finely chopped
1 teaspoon ground coriander
½ teaspoon ground turmeric
¼ teaspoon red chilli powder
2 cucumbers, halved lengthwise, deseeded and cut into 0.5cm half-moon slices
400ml coconut milk
1 teaspoon mango powder (*amchur*) or lemon juice
sea salt

Drain the cashew nuts and set aside.

Melt the coconut oil in a saucepan with a lid over a medium-high heat. Add the chillies, mustard seeds and cumin seeds, and fry, stirring, until the seeds pop and crackle. Add the curry leaves and onion with a pinch of salt, and fry, stirring often, until the onion becomes translucent. Add the ground coriander, ground turmeric and chilli powder, and stir for 30 seconds to cook the ground spices. Watch closely so they do not burn.

Stir in the cashew nuts and cucumbers with salt to taste, but remember the onion has already been salted. You want the nuts and cucumbers well coated in the spices. Add the coconut milk and mango powder and bring to the boil. Lower the heat and leave to simmer for 10 minutes, or until the cucumbers are tender and becoming translucent. Taste and adjust the salt, if necessary, and serve.

● atul's tip

The round red cascabel chillies are very common is southern Indian cooking, and I was able to find mine at a local shop. If you can't find these specific chillies, ordinary Kashmiri chillies will do.

The aromas of the spices and pulses cooking in coconut oil take me straight back to my days as a young chef in southern India. I still love these flavours, and this simple preparation, made with black mustard seeds and finished with lots of fresh coconut. I think a *thoran* makes a light addition to an Indian meal, providing a contrast to the richer curries. I hope you enjoy.

Spiced Beans & Coconut
achinea payar thoran

1 tablespoon coconut oil
1 teaspoon black mustard seeds
1 teaspoon dried split brown chickpeas (*channa daal* or Bengal gram)
1 teaspoon split white lentils (*urid daal*)
2.5cm piece of a large dried red chilli
¼ teaspoon ground fenugreek
8–10 fresh or dried curry leaves
150g French beans, topped and tailed and thinly sliced
½ teaspoon ground turmeric
4 tablespoons freshly grated coconut, plus a little extra, to garnish (see Atul's tip, below)
sea salt

Melt the coconut oil in a large frying pan over a medium-high heat. Add the mustard seeds and fry, stirring, until they pop. Add the split brown chickpeas, split white lentils and the chilli, and continue stirring until the pulses turn light brown. It is important to cook the pulses well at this stage, or you could end up with an upset stomach.

When the pulses begin to colour, stir in the ground fenugreek, then add the curry leaves and beans and stir. Add the turmeric and salt to taste and continue stirring for 30 seconds to cook the turmeric. By now the both pulses should be golden brown.

Continue stirring until the green beans are just al dente. Sprinkle with the coconut and stir everything together, then taste and adjust the salt, if necessary. Sprinkle with extra coconut and serve.

● atul's tip

While freshly grated coconut is readily available in southern India, it's not always that easy to find elsewhere. If that's the case, don't hesitate to use frozen grated coconut. It will quickly thaw in the residual heat in the pan.

Typical of many South Indian dishes, the spice powder in this recipe is a mix of spices and lentils, all of which are toasted before being ground. Traditionally this is served without any accompaniments other than yogurt or mint raita (page 292) on the side along with poppadoms.

Aubergine Rice
vanghi bhath

200g white basmati rice, rinsed under running cold water until the water runs clear, then left to soak in a bowl of fresh water for 30 minutes

2 tablespoons sunflower oil

5–6 fresh or dried curry leaves

1 tablespoon dried split brown chickpeas (*channa daal* or Bengal gram)

1 tablespoon coarsely chopped unsalted skinned peanuts, plus extra, to garnish, optional

1 teaspoon cumin seeds

1 teaspoon split white lentils (*urid daal*)

½ teaspoon black mustard seeds

1 onion, thinly sliced

½ long, thin green chilli

100g aubergine, trimmed and cut into bite-sized pieces

½ teaspoon ground turmeric

75g fresh or frozen peas

3 tablespoons tamarind extract (see Atul's tips, right)

sea salt

chopped coriander leaves, to garnish

First, cook the rice. Bring a saucepan of salted water to the boil. Drain the rice and add it to the boiling water and boil for 6–8 minutes, until tender. Drain well, rinse under cold running water, drain well again and spread out on a large plate to cool. Set aside until required.

Meanwhile, make the spice powder. Heat a dry frying pan over a medium heat. Add the coriander seeds and toast, stirring constantly, until they darken. Immediately tip them on to a plate. Add the split chickpeas and white split lentils to the pan and stir until they start to colour, then add the chillies and continue stirring until the lentils turn light brown. Immediately tip them on to the plate.

Add the cloves, desiccated coconut, cumin seeds, fenugreek seeds and cinnamon to the pan, and toast, stirring, until the seeds start to pop and the coconut turns light brown. Immediately tip out of the pan.

When all the toasted ingredients are cool, transfer them to a spice grinder, coffee grinder or pestle and mortar, and grind until a powder forms. Pass the powder through a fine sieve. Set aside.

When you are ready to start cooking, heat the oil in large frying pan with a lid over a medium-high heat. Add the curry leaves, split chickpeas, peanuts, cumin seeds, split white lentils and mustard seeds, and fry, stirring, until the seeds crackle and pop and the pulses start to darken. Add the onion and green

For the *vangi bhath* spice powder

2 tablespoons coriander seeds
1 tablespoon dried split brown chickpeas (*channa daal* or Bengal gram)
1½ teaspoons split white lentils (*urid daal*)
1–2 large flat dried red chillies, to taste
4 cloves
1 tablespoon desiccated coconut
1 teaspoon cumin seeds
¼ teaspoon fenugreek seeds
a small piece of cinnamon bark

chilli with a pinch of salt, and continue stirring until the onion is light golden brown. Keep an eye on the pan so none of the ingredients burn.

Add the aubergine, turmeric and a pinch of salt to taste to the pan, but remember the onion is already salted so you might not need much. Continue stirring for 30 seconds to cook the turmeric. Cover the pan and leave to steam-cook over a medium heat, stirring occasionally, for 8–10 minutes until the aubergine is tender.

Add the peas and stir the spice powder through the vegetables. Add the tamarind and continue stirring until the peas are hot.

Add the rice to the pan and stir everything together. Taste and adjust the salt, if necessary. Garnish with coriander leaves and extra peanuts, if you want. It's ready to serve.

atul's tips

I use tamarind extract regularly for its tangy, sour flavour. You can buy bottles of tamarind extract, but the extract can be salty, so I recommend you buy the seedless, dried, compressed blocks available from Asian supermarkets. Put a 200g block of pulp in a bowl, pour over about 400ml hot water and, when it's cool enough that you won't burn yourself, use your fingers to break up the pulp. The liquid becomes darker and thicker as the pulp dissolves. After all the pulp has dissolved, strain it into a clean glass jar, screw on the lid and store in the fridge for 2–3 weeks. Alternatively, it can be frozen and defrosted as required.

For a milder flavour, dilute tamarind paste with water to make tamarind water. I use two parts water to one part paste.

A common misconception outside India is that a *korma* is a mildly spiced curry. The word '*korma*' actually refers to the cooking technique, which in Hindi and Urdu means 'to braise', and you will come across both mild and highly spiced *kormas*.

Cauliflower Korma
gobi korma

2 tablespoons sunflower oil
   or coconut oil
3–4 green cardamom pods,
   bruised, to taste
2 cloves
1 dried bay leaf
1 star anise
½ teaspoon cumin seeds
½ teaspoon crushed fennel
   seeds (page 270)
a small piece of cinnamon bark
1 onion, finely chopped
½ long, thin green chilli, sliced
   lengthwise
2 teaspoons Ginger-Garlic Paste
   (page 281)
1 tomato, chopped
½ teaspoon red chilli powder
½ teaspoon ground turmeric
¼ teaspoon garam masala
130g peeled carrots, diced
75g cauliflower florets
150g frozen peas
sea salt
chopped coriander leaves,
   to garnish

For the cashew-coconut paste
60g unsalted cashew nuts
50g fresh coconut chips or
   frozen grated coconut
120ml water

First make the cashew-coconut paste. Put the cashew nuts, coconut and water in a food processor, and process until a thin, smooth paste forms. Set aside.

Heat the oil in a large frying pan with a lid over a medium-high heat. Add the cardamom pods, cloves, bay leaf, star anise, cumin seeds, fennel seeds and cinnamon, and fry, stirring, until the spices crackle. Add the onion and chilli and continue stirring until the onion turns light brown. Add the ginger-garlic paste and continue stirring for 1 minute so the raw flavour doesn't linger. If the paste doesn't get cooked at this point, it never will.

Stir in the tomato, then add the red chilli powder, turmeric, garam masala and ½ teaspoon salt, and stir for a further 30 seconds to cook the spices. Watch closely so they don't burn.

Add the cashew-coconut paste and reduce the heat to medium, otherwise the paste can catch and burn quite quickly. Add a couple tablespoons of water to the spice grinder and swirl around to get all the flavour, then set on the side of the hob to use if the ingredients start sticking. Stir, scraping up the browned bits from the bottom of the pan, for about 1 minute, so the paste is well cooked.

Stir in the carrots and cauliflower florets so they are well coated. Stir in the reserved water in the spice grinder, then add enough water to just cover the vegetables. Cover the pan and bring to the boil. Reduce the heat and leave the vegetables to simmer for 15 minutes, or until al dente.

Uncover, stir in the peas and leave to simmer for 2–3 minutes until the peas are hot and the carrot and cauliflower are tender. Taste and adjust the salt, if necessary. Garnish with coriander and serve.

● atul's tip

In the restaurants, we sauté the spices and prepare the gravy – making sure the ginger-garlic paste is well cooked – and blanch all the vegetables in advance. That way when an order comes in, we add the vegetables to the sautéed spices and put the gravy on top to bring the dish together. This is a good way to prepare this dish for a dinner party when you don't want to be stuck in the kitchen while your guests are enjoying pre-dinner drinks.

Serves 4 as a sharing dish

I have always loved eating beetroot, but I never got to see or try beetroot leaves until I moved to the UK. These days, I grow my own beetroots and relish the whole vegetable – its leaves, stalks and roots. It is one of my favourite ingredients, which is very unusual for an Indian!

Green Leaves & Coconut Stir-fry
chukunder ke patte aur nariyal ka saag

2 tablespoons coconut oil
1 teaspoon black mustard seeds
¼ teaspoon fenugreek seeds
1 tablespoon dried split brown chickpeas (*channa daal* or Bengal gram)
1 teaspoon split white lentils (*urid daal*)
1 dried red chilli, cut in half
15–20 fresh curry leaves
1 onion, chopped
1 tablespoon finely chopped fresh ginger
¼ teaspoon ground turmeric
½ teaspoon red chilli powder
800g spinach, beetroot or mixed green leaves and stalks, shredded and rinsed
200g fresh or frozen grated coconut
4 tablespoons coconut milk
sea salt

Melt the coconut oil in a wok or large frying pan over a medium-high heat. Add the mustard seeds and fenugreek seeds and stir until they pop and turn darker. Add the split chickpeas and stir until they darken slightly, which will happen very quickly. Add the white split lentils and continue stirring for a further 30 seconds.

Add the red chilli, followed by the curry leaves and onion. Lower the heat a little and fry, stirring often, until the onion turns light brown. Stir in the ginger, turmeric and chilli powder, then add the beetroot leaves and stalks. Continue stirring until the leaves start to wilt. Season with salt to taste, add the coconut and continue stir-frying for a further 5–6 minutes until coconut becomes caramelised.

Drizzle over the coconut milk and stir well. Adjust the salt, if necessary. It's ready to serve.

Usually this simple, semi-dry dish from Tamil Nadu is made with green cabbage, but I wanted to give it my own twist by using red cabbage. *Kootus* like this can be made with many vegetables, but they always consist of one vegetable and one toasted dal. Serve with freshly boiled basmati rice (page 283) and parathas (page 289).

Warm Red Cabbage Salad
muttaikkos kootu

200g dried split brown chickpeas (*channa daal* or Bengal gram), rinsed and soaked in water to cover for 20 minutes
180g red cabbage, cored and finely chopped
4 fresh or dried curry leaves
1 teaspoon ground turmeric
4 tablespoons tamarind extract (see Atul's tip, page 167)
sea salt

For the toasted coconut-chickpea paste
2 tablespoons dried split brown chickpeas (*channa daal* or Bengal gram)
1 teaspoon cumin seeds
½ dried red chilli
100g fresh or frozen grated coconut (see Atul's tips, right)
200ml water

For the tarka
1½ tablespoons coconut oil
¼ teaspoon asafoetida
12 fresh or dried curry leaves
1 teaspoon black mustard seeds

Drain the split chickpeas, then transfer them to a saucepan a lid with fresh water to cover and salt to taste, and bring to the boil. Partially cover the pan, and simmer for 20 minutes, or until they are cooked just a bit more than al dente, but not so tender that they fall apart. Stir in extra water if they get too dry. Set aside without draining.

Meanwhile, make the toasted coconut-chickpea paste. Heat a dry frying pan over a medium heat. Add the dry split chickpeas, cumin seeds and dried red chilli, and stir until the chickpeas are golden brown. Immediately tip them and the spices out of the pan.

Add the coconut to the dry pan, and stir over a medium-high until it turns light brown. Tip out of the pan and leave to cool.

When all the toasted ingredients are cool, transfer them to a blender or food processor with the water and process until a thick paste forms. Set aside.

Return the pan with the cooked chickpeas and their cooking water to a medium-high heat. Stir in the red cabbage, curry leaves, turmeric and salt to taste, and bring to the boil, stirring occasionally. Leave to simmer until most of the liquid evaporates.

Add the coconut-chickpea paste and the tamarind extract and stir over medium-high heat until the mixture returns to the boil. Leave to simmer, stirring occasionally and watching to ensure that the paste doesn't stick to the bottom of the pan, until the dish has a semi-dry consistency. Taste and adjust the salt, if necessary.

Just before you're ready to serve, make the tarka. Melt the coconut oil in a frying pan over a medium-high heat. Add the asafoetida and stir until it foams and subsides. Add the curry leaves and mustard seeds and fry, stirring, until the seeds pop.

Pour the tarka into the pan of split chickpeas and stir together. As the dish cools, it will continue to thicken.

● atul's tips

There's nothing like fresh coconut, but frozen grated coconut works perfectly fine in this recipe. Use it straight from the freezer and toast as above, but it will just take a little longer to colour. Do not, however, make this with desiccated coconut.

For a vegetarian dish, rather than this vegan version, you could replace the coconut oil in the tarka with ghee.

There are many recipes for *bharwa baingan*, however this one is the one closest to my heart. You can enjoy it as it is but I think that aubergines and tomatoes are a winning combination so you could serve it with a simple spiced tomato sauce using cumin, ginger, garlic, garam masala, salt and lemon juice.

Stuffed Baby Aubergines
bharwa baingan

8 baby aubergines
4 tablespoons sunflower oil
¼ teaspoon ground asafoetida
1 teaspoon cumin seeds
1 teaspoon black mustard seeds
sea salt
pea shoots or chopped
    coriander leaves, to garnish

For the spice stuffing
10g unsalted skinned peanuts
150g tomatoes, deseeded and
    finely chopped
1 garlic clove, chopped
1 tablespoon chickpea flour
    (*besan*)
1 tablespoon finely chopped
    coriander leaves
1 teaspoon ground cumin
1 teaspoon ground coriander
1 teaspoon sugar
½ teaspoon mango powder
    (*amchur*) or lemon juice
¼ teaspoon red chilli powder
¼ teaspoon garam masala

Preheat the oven to 200°C/Fan 180°C/Gas 6. Slice each aubergine lengthways, without cutting all the way through, to create a pocket for the stuffing when you gently squeeze from both ends. Set aside.

To make the spice stuffing, begin by toasting the peanuts. Put them in a dry frying pan over a medium-high heat and stir for about 1 minute until lightly browned. Remove from the pan and leave to cool, then transfer to a spice grinder or coffee grinder, or use a pestle and mortar, and grind until finely ground. Put the ground peanuts in a bowl with the remaining spice stuffing ingredients and a pinch of salt to taste, and mix together. Equally divide the stuffing among the aubergines, adding about 1 tablespoon to each. Transfer the aubergines to a roasting tin, stuffed sides up, then set aside.

Heat the sunflower oil in a frying pan over a medium-high heat. Add the asafoetida and stir until it foams and subsides. Add the cumin seeds and mustard seeds and fry, stirring, until the seeds crackle and pop. Pour the oil and seeds over the aubergines, then cover the roasting tin with kitchen foil, shiny side down.

Roast the aubergines for 40 minutes, basting with the oil in the tin once during cooking. Remove the foil, baste again and roast for a further 5 minutes, or until the aubergines are very tender. Sprinkle with pea shoots or coriander and serve.

This recipe comes from the state of Maharashtra, which grows chillies, cloves and black peppercorns on a large scale, all reflected in this hot and spicy dish. I've included two large dried red chillies in the spice powder for authenticity, but feel free to cut back if you prefer. Serve this as a side dish with freshly boiled basmati rice (page 283) and some protein, such a paneer of tofu. A cooling mint raita (page 292) is a good idea, too.

Pumpkin & Green Mango Curry
bhopla ani amba kari

1½ tablespoons sunflower oil
2cm piece of fresh ginger, peeled and chopped
½ long, thin green chilli
½ teaspoon ground turmeric
400g pumpkin or butternut squash, peeled, deseeded and cut into bite-sized pieces
1 small green mango, halved, stoned, inner membrane removed, flesh removed and chopped
250ml water
50g fresh or frozen grated coconut
1 tablespoon chopped coriander leaves
sea salt

For the Malvani curry powder
2 large flat, dried chillies
1 teaspoon cumin seeds
1 teaspoon fennel seeds
½ teaspoon coriander seeds
½ teaspoon fenugreek seeds
½ teaspoon black peppercorns

First, make the curry powder. Heat a dry frying pan over a medium heat. Add the chillies and stir until they start to darken. Immediately tip them out of the pan. Continue to toast each seed and the peppercorns individually until they start to pop or become aromatic. The pan is hot, so it won't take long, but watch closely, to prevent them burning.

When all the toasted ingredients are cool, transfer them to a spice grinder or coffee grinder, or use a pestle and mortar, and grind until a powder forms. If using a pestle and mortar, pass through a fine sieve. Set aside.

Heat the oil in a large frying pan with a lid over a medium-high heat. And the ginger and green chilli and fry, stirring, until the ginger turns light brown, watching closely so it doesn't burn. Stir in the ground turmeric and curry powder and continue stirring for 30 seconds. Add the pumpkin, mango and salt to taste, and give everything a good stir. Stir in the water, cover the pan and bring to the boil. Reduce the heat and leave to simmer for about 10 minutes, stirring occasionally, until the pumpkin is tender.

Stir in the coconut and coriander. If you are using frozen coconut, stir until it thaws and becomes hot. Taste and adjust the salt, if necessary, and serve.

This was my favourite recipe during the first national Covid lockdown of 2020. While everyone was at home, restricted and not being able to do much, with few fresh groceries and limited access to the food shops, I think we were cooking more and experimenting with the ingredients in our pantries. I had a few cans of three-bean salad that I wanted to make a good use of, hence this recipe.

Eggs & Curried Bean Salad
beans pe eedu

3 tablespoons rapeseed oil
4 teaspoons coriander seeds
1½ teaspoons cumin seeds
¾ teaspoon black peppercorns
5 garlic cloves, chopped
3 celery sticks, chopped
2 onions, chopped
2 x 400g cans three-bean salad, drained and rinsed
3 large tomatoes, chopped
1½ teaspoons ground coriander
¾ teaspoon ground turmeric
¼–½ teaspoon red chilli powder, to taste
½ teaspoon garam masala
6 tablespoons passata
8 eggs
4 slices Cheddar cheese
sea salt
chopped coriander leaves, to garnish

Heat the oil in a large frying pan with a lid over a medium-high heat. Add the coriander seeds, cumin seeds and peppercorns, and fry, stirring, until they are fragrant and the cumin seeds crackle. Add the garlic, celery and onions, and continue stirring until the onions are translucent. Watch closely so nothing catches and burns.

Stir in the three-bean salad and the tomatoes. Reduce the heat to low and leave to simmer, stirring occasionally, for 5 minutes, or until the tomatoes are soft.

Stir in all the ground spices with salt to taste and continue stirring for 30 seconds to cook the spices. Stir in the passata.

Use the back of the spoon to make 8 indentations in the surface of the mixture, then crack in the eggs, one by one. Cover the pan and leave to simmer until the egg whites are just set and the yolks are still soft.

Tear the cheese into smaller pieces, place them on top of the eggs and re-cover the pan. Simmer for a further 2–3 minutes until the cheese melts. Serve hot, sprinkled with chopped coriander.

Parsi food has its own culinary footprint, and the journey of people of Parsi origin from Persia to India is full of gastronomic stories. I grew up Jamshedpur, in East India. It is an industrial centre, drawing workers from all over the country, which is how I was exposed to Parsi cooking from western Indian from an early age. Their meat cooking is amazing, but their vegetarian food is nothing short of fabulous, with such a mix of exciting flavours. This recipe is my homage to the fantastic Parsi community of Jamshedpur.

Potato & Spinach Curry
papeta ne palak ni tarkari

1 tablespoon rapeseed oil
2 garlic cloves, thinly sliced
500g floury potatoes, such as King Edwards, peeled and cut into 2cm wedges
2 tablespoons Parsi Masala (page 275)
400ml water
2 large tomatoes, each cut into 8 wedges
500g baby spinach leaves, rinsed
1 teaspoon ground toasted cumin seeds (page 270)
¼ teaspoon ground black pepper
sea salt

Heat a large wok over a medium-high heat. Add the oil and swirl it around. Add the garlic and stir-fry until it is lightly coloured. Add the potato wedges and fry, stirring occasionally, for 2–3 minutes. Add the Parsi masala and continue stirring for 30 seconds to coat the potatoes. Keep your eyes on the wok the whole time, because it can all catch and burn quickly.

Stir in the water with a pinch of salt to taste and bring to the boil, stirring. Reduce the heat and simmer for 12–15 minutes, turning the potatoes occasionally, until they are tender. Add more water, if necessary, to cover the potatoes and prevent them from sticking to the bottom of the pan.

Add the tomato wedges and continue simmering, stirring occasionally, for 3–5 minutes, until the tomatoes are soft. At this stage, most of the liquid will have evaporated. Stir in the spinach leaves with any water still clinging to their leaves, and mix well over a high heat until they wilt. Taste and adjust the salt, if necessary. Stir in the ground cumin seeds and black pepper. It's ready to serve.

Nepal might be much smaller than neighbouring India, but it holds it own when it comes to home-cooking. There are some clear culinary differences in the beautiful country, but I like to divide it based on the cuisine of mountains and the cuisine of plains. This is a straightforward recipe enjoyed throughout the country, with an added touch of the flavours from the Kathmandu Valley. Serve this with chapatis (page 288).

Pickled Potatoes
aloo achaar

400g new potatoes, scrubbed
50g black sesame seeds
2 tablespoons mustard oil
  (I use a blend of mustard oil
  and rapeseed oil available in
  supermarkets) or rapeseed oil
2 long, thin green chillies,
  thinly sliced
½ teaspoon red chilli powder
½ teaspoon Nepalese Garam
  Masala (page 271)
½ teaspoon ground turmeric
2 tablespoons freshly squeezed
  lemon juice
sea salt
chopped coriander leaves,
  to garnish, optional

Put the potatoes in a large saucepan of salted water over a high heat. Bring to the boil and boil for 15–20 minutes until tender. Drain well and set aside until cool enough to handle, then peel and set aside.

Meanwhile, heat a large, dry wok over a high heat. Add the sesame seeds and stir until they start to pop and become aromatic. Immediately tip them out of the pan to cool, then grind to a fine powder.

Add the oil to a wok over a high heat and swirl around, then reduce the heat to medium-high. Add the potatoes and sesame powder with the green chillies, red chilli powder, garam masala, turmeric and salt to taste, and stir-fry until the potatoes are well coated and the ground spices are cooked. Watch closely so the spices do not burn.

Stir in the lemon juice, taste and adjust the salt, if necessary. Sprinkle with coriander leaves and serve.

The Nepalese word *bhutuwa* means 'fried' or 'stir-fried'; in Hindi, it means 'ghostly' – but, there's no connection, I promise you! Throughout Nepal there are numerous vegetarian *bhutuwa* recipes made with local cheese, paneer, tofu, sweetcorn, onions and a many more ingredients, but cooking with greens is my favourite option. Some people also add soy sauce in these dishes, especially those that contain tofu or paneer, but I've decided to leave it out of this version. As well as making *bhutuwas* with mustard greens, I have also used kale, spinach, mixed greens and Brussels sprout tops, all equally successful.

Stir-fried Mustard Greens

sarson saag bhutuwa

2 tablespoons mustard oil (I use a blend of mustard oil and rapeseed oil available in supermarkets) or rapeseed oil
½ teaspoon ajwain seeds
½ teaspoon cumin seeds
½ teaspoon black mustard seeds
1 dried red chilli, crushed
1.5cm piece of fresh ginger, peeled and chopped
3 garlic cloves, chopped
½ teaspoon ground turmeric
½ teaspoon timur (*timut*) peppercorns or Szechuan peppercorns
500g mustard greens or mixed greens, shredded and rinsed
2 tablespoons finely chopped fresh dill
½ teaspoon freshly ground black pepper
¼ teaspoon Nepalese Garam Masala (page 271)
sea salt

Heat a large wok over a high heat. Add the oil and swirl it around. Add the ajwain seeds, cumin seeds and mustard seeds, and stir-fry until they crackle and pop. Add the dried chilli and continue stirring until the pieces darken.

Reduce the heat. Add the ginger, garlic, turmeric and timur peppercorns, and stir-fry for 1 minute to flavour the oil and cook the ginger and garlic. Watch closely so they do not burn.

Increase the heat to high again. Add the greens, season with salt to taste and stir-fry until the greens are wilted and the excess liquid has evaporated. Take care not overcook the greens.

Sprinkle over the chopped dill, black pepper and garam masala, then taste and adjust the salt, if necessary. It's ready to serve.

Left: Pickled Potatoes (page 182)
Right: A Stir-fry from the
Nepalese Plains (page 186)
Bottom: Stir-fried Mustard
Greens (page 183)

Serves 4

Choila is a popular, spicy, fresh recipe that also works well as a filling for flatbread rolls and tacos. The zing comes from the timur (*timut*) pepper, which has the same mouth-tingling character of Chinese Szechuan pepper.

A Stir-fry from the Nepalese Plains
tarai ko choila

500g tempeh, firm tofu, seitan or paneer, drained and patted dry, if necessary, and cut into 2.5cm cubes
3 tablespoons rapeseed oil
1 teaspoon cumin seeds
½ teaspoon fenugreek seeds
2 fresh red bird's-eye chillies, thinly sliced
1.5cm piece of fresh ginger, peeled and finely chopped
2 garlic cloves, finely chopped
1 onion, finely chopped
½ teaspoon ground turmeric
¼ teaspoon red chilli powder
a small pinch of timur (*timut*) peppercorns, finely ground, or ground Szechuan pepper
6 spring onions, thinly sliced
2 tomatoes, finely chopped
2 tablespoons finely chopped coriander leaves
2 tablespoons freshly squeezed lemon juice
sea salt and freshly ground black pepper

For the marinade
1 tablespoon freshly squeezed lemon juice
1 tablespoon rapeseed oil
½ teaspoon red chilli powder
½ teaspoon ground turmeric

Mix all the marinade ingredients together in a non-metallic bowl with salt and pepper to taste. Add the tempeh and toss until well coated. Cover and chill for at least 1 hour, or overnight.

Preheat the grill to high, or heat a cast-iron, ridged griddle pan over a high heat. If using the grill, line the grill rack with foil. Put the tempeh pieces on the grill rack, or in the grill pan, and cook for about 10 minutes, turning them over occasionally, until browned on all sides. Set aside.

When you're ready to cook, heat a large wok over a high heat. Add the oil and swirl it around. Add the cumin and fenugreek seeds and stir-fry until the cumin seeds crackle and the fenugreek seeds turn darker. Add the bird's-eye chillies, ginger and garlic, and stir-fry until the garlic turns light brown. Watch closely, because the ingredients can catch and burn quickly.

Add the onion and continue stir-frying until it is translucent. Add the ground turmeric, chilli powder and timur pepper, and stir-fry for a further 30 seconds to cook the ground spices.

Add the tempeh to the wok with any remaining marinade and gently stir to mix well with the onions and spices. Add the spring onions, tomatoes, coriander leaves, lemon juice and salt to taste, and stir well before serving.

I love this recipe. It has all the rich umami flavour that one craves – and just the right amount of subtle spicing. I know it looks like a small amount of Nepalese garam masala, but try the recipe as I've written it before you're tempted to add more. You can use canned beans, if you wish to – but that's not a short-cut I would take. I serve this with freshly boiled basmati rice (page 283).

Bamboo Shoot, Potato & Black-eye Bean Curry
aloo tama bodi

250g dried black-eye beans, rinsed and soaked for at least 6 hours, or overnight, in cold water to cover

3 tablespoons rapeseed oil

6–8 timur (*timut*) peppercorns or Szechuan peppercorns

1 teaspoon cumin seeds

¼ teaspoon fenugreek seeds

4 garlic cloves, finely chopped

2 onions, thinly sliced

2 floury potatoes, such as King Edwards, peeled and cut into 1cm cubes

1 tablespoon ground coriander

1 teaspoon ground cumin

1 teaspoon ground turmeric

½ teaspoon red chilli powder

¼ teaspoon Nepalese Garam Masala (page 271)

3 tomatoes, blended to a paste

2 x 227g cans bamboo shoots or fermented bamboo shoots, drained

1 litre water or vegetable stock, ideally home-made (page 282)

sea salt

Drain the beans and rinse. Place them in a large saucepan with a lid with cold water to cover, then cover the pan and bring to the boil. Uncover the pan and boil hard for 10 minutes, then drain well, rinse and set aside. Wash and dry the pan.

Heat the oil in the pan over a medium-high heat. Add the peppercorns, cumin seeds and fenugreek seeds, and stir until the cumin seeds crackle and the fenugreek seeds turn darker. Add the garlic and onions and fry, stirring often, until the onions are light brown. Watch closely so the garlic does not catch and burn.

Add the potatoes and stir for 1 minute to coat them in the spices. Stir in the drained black-eye beans, then add the ground coriander, cumin, turmeric, chilli powder and Nepalese garam masala with salt to taste, and stir for 30 seconds to cook the spices. Watch closely so they do not burn.

Add the blended tomatoes, bamboo shoots and water, and bring to the boil, stirring. Reduce the heat and simmer gently for 35 minutes, stirring occasionally and adding a splash of water, if necessary, or until the beans are tender. Taste and adjust the salt, if necessary. It's ready to serve.

Serves 6–8

Because Nepal and Tibet share a border, Tibet's influence on Nepalese food is unmistakable, which is why this warming soup contains noodles – it's a hearty meal in a bowl.

Vegetable Noodle Soup
tarkari thukpa

200g Tibetan noodles, dried thin rice noodles or thin egg noodles
1 tablespoon rapeseed oil, plus extra for the noodles
¼ teaspoon ajwain seeds
1.5cm piece of fresh ginger, peeled and chopped
3 garlic cloves, chopped
2 long, thin green chillies, thinly sliced
1 onion, finely chopped
2 tomatoes, chopped
100g carrot, peeled and finely diced
100g small cauliflower florets
100g green beans, topped and tailed and finely chopped
100g fresh or frozen peas
1 teaspoon ground turmeric
½ teaspoon ground cumin
1 litre vegetable stock, ideally home-made (page 282)
200g baby spinach leaves, shredded and rinsed
2 tablespoons soy sauce
sea salt and freshly ground black pepper
chopped coriander leaves, to garnish

Bring a large saucepan of salted water to the boil. Add the noodles and cook according to the packet instructions until they are just al dente – you don't want them completely cooked at this point because they will simmer in stock. Drain well and rinse under cold water to stop them cooking any further. Drain again, toss very lightly in oil to prevent them sticking and set aside.

Heat the oil in a large saucepan over a medium-high heat. Add the ajwain seeds and stir until they crackle. Add the ginger, garlic, green chillies and onion with a small pinch of salt, and fry, stirring often, until the onions are translucent. Add the tomatoes, carrot, cauliflower, green beans and peas, and continue stirring for 2–3 minutes.

Add the turmeric and ground cumin and stir for 30 seconds to cook the ground spices. Add the vegetable stock, spinach leaves and soy sauce, and bring to the boil. Reduce the heat and simmer for 5 minutes, or until all the vegetables are tender and the flavours blended. Taste and adjust the salt, if necessary.

Over a low heat, stir the noodles into the pan and continue simmering until they are cooked to your liking. Sprinkle with coriander leaves and serve.

Similar to Chinese *baozis* and Japanese *gyozas*, these steamed dumplings crossed into Nepal from Tibet, and they have become naturalised with the addition of garlic and fenugreek seeds for flavouring. I serve these with tomato salsa (page 292), but use whatever chutney or dipping sauce you like – the *nuoc cham* (page 51) would also be good.

Vegetable Dumplings
tarkari ko momo

2 tablespoons rapeseed oil, plus extra for greasing the steamer rack
½ teaspoon fenugreek seeds
2 onions, very finely chopped
2.5cm piece of fresh ginger, very finely chopped
2 fresh red chillies, very finely chopped
1 garlic clove, very finely chopped
½ teaspoon ground turmeric
600g mixed vegetables of your choice, such as carrots, cauliflower florets, courgettes, green beans, fresh or frozen peas, red and green peppers, prepared as necessary and all very finely chopped
200g firm tofu or Nepalese cheese (paneer), grated
200g spring onions, very finely chopped
2 tablespoons finely chopped coriander leaves
½ teaspoon timur (*timut*) peppercorns, finely ground, or use ground Szechuan pepper
½ teaspoon ground black pepper

Heat a large wok over a medium-high heat. Add the oil and swirl it around. Add the fenugreek seeds and stir-fry until they turn darker. Add the onions and continue stir-frying until they are lightly browned. Add the ginger, red chillies, garlic and turmeric, and continue stir-frying until fragrant.

Reduce the heat to medium. Add the prepared vegetables with salt to taste and continue stir-frying until they are all tender.

Stir in the tofu, spring onions and coriander, then season with the ground timur peppercorns and salt and black pepper to taste, and mix well. Add the cornflour paste and stir for 1 minute to cook the cornflour and thicken the mixture. Remove the wok from the heat and leave the filling to cool completely.

To make the dough, put the flour and a pinch of salt in a large bowl and make a well in the centre. Add the water and oil and knead into a soft dough. Cover with a damp tea towel and leave to rest for 40 minutes at room temperature.

Tip the dough on to a lightly floured work surface and knead again until smooth. Shape the dough into about forty-eight 2.5cm balls. Working with one ball at a time, and using a lightly floured rolling pin, roll each ball into a 7.5cm disc. Place 1 tablespoon

1 tablespoon cornflour mixed
  with 2 tablespoons water to
  make a thin paste
sea salt
chilli flakes, to garnish

For the dough
500g plain flour, plus extra
  for rolling out
200ml water
1 tablespoon rapeseed oil

filling in the centre of each disc, then moisten the edge. Gather the dough around the filling and pinch together at the top to make a dumpling in the shape of a 'moneybag'. Set aside on a floured baking tray or plate, cover with a damp tea towel and continue until all the dough discs are filled.

If you are using a metal steamer, brush the rack with oil; if you are using a bamboo steamer, line the rack with greaseproof paper. Place the dumplings in the steamer and place over boiling water, making sure the water doesn't touch the bottom of the steamer you are using. Cover and steam for around 8–10 minutes until the pastry becomes transparent and is cooked through. Cook the dumplings in batches, if necessary, topping up the water and making sure it is boiling before adding a new batch.

Garnish with chilli flakes and serve the hot dumplings with tomato salsa on the side.

atul's tips

This recipe probably makes more dumplings than you want for one meal, but when I make them at home I make enough to freeze for a second meal. They are a good stand-by to have in the freezer because they can be steamed from frozen.

If you don't want to use a steamer, as I've suggested in this recipe, these dumplings can also be pan-fried like the pot-stickers on page 224.

'Vegetable curry' must be the most maligned culinary phrase, conjuring up an image of boring vegetables in a thin, spicy broth. This Nepalese curry will change your perception forever; it has a light touch of spice with an abundance of full vegetable flavours. I serve this with basmati rice (page 283) and/or chapatis (page 288).

Nepalese Vegetable Curry
nepal ma banaiko tarkari

3 tablespoons rapeseed oil
2 garlic cloves, grated or crushed
1 onion, thinly sliced
1cm piece of fresh ginger, peeled and grated
300g floury potatoes, such as King Edwards, peeled and cut into 1cm cubes
2 teaspoons ground coriander
1 teaspoon red chilli powder
1 teaspoon ground cumin
¼ teaspoon ground turmeric
100g fresh bamboo shoots, peeled and chopped, or 1 can (227g) bamboo shoots, drained
500g mixed vegetables of your choice, such as asparagus, broccoli, carrots, courgettes, green beans, fresh or frozen peas, red peppers and pumpkin, prepared as required and diced
1 tomato, chopped
100ml water
½ teaspoon Nepalese Garam Masala (page 271)
sea salt
chopped coriander leaves, to garnish

Heat the oil in a large saucepan with a lid over a medium heat. Add the garlic, onion and ginger, and fry, stirring often, until the onion is light brown. Add the potatoes and stir until they are well coated. Stir in the ground coriander, chilli powder, ground cumin and turmeric, and continue stirring for 30 seconds to cook the ground spices.

Add the bamboo shoots and prepared vegetables to the pan, and fry, stirring often, for 2 minutes to seal them. Add the tomato, water and a pinch of salt.

Bring to the boil, then cover the pan, lower the heat and simmer for 8–10 minutes until all the vegetables are tender. Taste and adjust the salt, if necessary, then sprinkle with the garam masala. Garnish with coriander leaves and serve.

● **atul's tip**

For an exotic touch to this simple curry, look for fiddleheads, the unfurled fern leaves treated as a vegetable in Nepal. You are unlikely to find them fresh outside North America or in the Asian countries, but frozen and bottled ones can be used in this recipe.

Sri Lanka has a sizeable Tamil population because of its vicinity to India's southern border. Not surprisingly, there are quite lot of similarities in the cuisines, but Sri Lankan cooks have their own spice combinations. The toasted Sri Lankan spice powder in this recipe is an amazing addition to your spice cupboard, and it's so versatile – add it sparingly to your biscuit recipes. Traditional accompaniments for this curry include Aubergine Salad (page 197), hoppers (page 186), chapatis (page 288) or boiled basmati rice (page 283).

Chickpea Curry
kandy kadala kari

2 tablespoons coconut oil
2.5cm piece of cinnamon bark
4 green cardamom pods, bruised
2 cloves
1 dried bay leaf
1 teaspoon cumin seeds
10 fresh or dried curry leaves
2 onions, thinly sliced
1 long, thin green chilli, thinly sliced
1 tablespoon Ginger-Garlic Paste (page 281)
2 tomatoes, deseeded and blended to a paste
1 tablespoon Sri Lankan Toasted Curry Powder (page 272)
½ teaspoon ground turmeric
600g cooked chickpeas, drained and rinsed if canned
200ml water
100ml coconut milk
sea salt
1 tablespoon chopped coriander leaves

Heat a wok over a medium-high heat. Add the coconut oil and swirl it around until it melts. Add the cinnamon bark, cardamom pods, cloves, bay leaf and cumin seeds, and stir-fry until the spices begin to crackle and pop. Add the curry leaves, onions and green chilli with a pinch of salt, and continue stir-frying until the onions turn translucent. Add the ginger-garlic paste and stir for a further minute to cook out the rawness.

Add the tomatoes, curry powder and ground turmeric, and stir-fry for a further 30 seconds to cook the ground spices. Stir in the chickpeas and water. Bring to a boil, then lower the heat and simmer for 12–15 minutes for the flavours to blend.

Stir in the coconut milk and simmer for a further 2–3 minutes, stirring. Finish by stirring in the chopped coriander leaves. Taste and adjust the salt, if necessary, then serve.

Sambols, a type of Sri Lankan salad, are made with various ingredients and they are meant to be eaten alongside a main course, not as a meal in itself. The lime juice in this simple dish is essential to counter the sweetness of the carrot. Like all *sambols*, this is best served at room temperature soon after preparing to capture the fresh flavours. I particularly like to serve with rice and a curry, such as Red Lentil Curry with Spinach (page 202).

Carrot Salad
carrot sambol

2 tablespoons freshly squeezed
  lime juice
300g carrots, peeled and grated
1 red onion, finely chopped
1 tomato, chopped
100g fresh or frozen grated
  coconut, thawed if frozen and
  patted dry
2 long, thin green chillies,
  thinly sliced
sea salt and freshly ground
  black pepper
fresh coriander, to serve

Season the lime juice with salt and pepper to taste and set aside.

Put the carrots, red onion, tomato, and coconut in a non-metallic serving bowl. Drizzle with the lime juice dressing, then mix together. Taste and adjust the salt, if necessary. Scatter with coriander and it's ready to serve.

Serves 4–6 as a sharing dish

This is quite a summery salad. The thin aubergine slices are fried and mixed with onions and chillies for a piquant flavour. Sometimes salad leaves are tossed through, and I suggest doing that in this recipe for a little crunch. This salad is an excellent side dish to serve with a traditional Sri Lankan meal of curry and rice.

Aubergine Salad
brinijal sambol

400g small aubergines
1 tablespoon rice flour
¼ teaspoon ground turmeric
vegetable oil, for deep-frying
finely grated zest of 1 lime and
   3 tablespoons freshly
   squeezed juice
1½ teaspoons sugar
1 long, thin green chilli,
   thinly sliced
1 large red onion, thinly sliced
1 large tomato, deseeded
   and sliced
1 teaspoon red chilli flakes
a small handful of coriander
   sprigs
Baby Gem lettuce leaves, cut
   or torn into small pieces and
   rinsed, optional
sea salt

Cut the aubergines in half lengthwise and then into thin slices. Put the slices in a bowl, add the rice flour, turmeric and a pinch of salt, and toss together. Set aside.

Heat enough vegetable oil for deep-frying in a deep-fat fryer or heavy-based saucepan to 180°C, and line a baking tray with kitchen paper.

Add as many aubergine slices to the oil that will fit without overcrowding the pan and deep-fry until golden brown all over. Use a slotted spoon to transfer them to the tray and spread out to keep them crisp. Fry in batches, if necessary, and reheat the oil to the correct temperature between batches.

In a non-metallic bowl, whisk the lime zest and juice with the sugar and a pinch of salt. Stir in the green chilli, red onion, tomato, chilli flakes, coriander sprigs, Baby Gem leaves, if using, and the crisp aubergine slices. Serve immediately.

Top left: Chickpea
Curry (page 195)
Top right: Aubergine
Salad (page 197)
Bottom left: Stir-fried
Kale with Coconut
(page 200)
Bottom right: Carrot
Salad (page 196)

Mallung, or *mallum*, translates as a shredded lightly cooked green vegetable with grated coconut that is flavoured with spices and fresh chilli or black pepper. It's an essential part of Sri Lankan meals and has proven nutritional benefits. Garlic, curry leaves and watercress are other strong flavours that can be used in the seasoning. This goes well with any Sri Lankan curry and lots of freshly boiled basmati rice (page 283).

Stir-fried Kale with Coconut
kale mallung

2 tablespoons coconut oil
½ teaspoon black mustard seeds
½ teaspoon split white lentils
  (*urid daal*)
1 dried red chilli, broken into
  small pieces
1 long thin green chilli,
  thinly sliced
1 large red onion, chopped
200g kale, hard core removed
  with the leaves thinly sliced,
  well rinsed and drained
½ teaspoon ground turmeric
3 tablespoons frozen grated
  coconut
1 tablespoon freshly squeezed
  lemon juice, or to taste
sea salt

Heat a large wok over a medium-high heat. Add the coconut oil and swirl it around as it melts. Add the mustard seeds and split white lentils and stir-fry until the mustard seeds pop and the lentils turn light brown. Lower the heat, add the dried red chilli and let it swell and darken.

Turn the heat back up to medium-high. Add the green chilli and onion and continue stir-frying until the onion turns light brown. Keep your eye on the wok so nothing catches and burns.

Add the kale and stir-fry for 4–5 minutes until it wilts. Add the turmeric and salt to taste and stir-fry for about 30 seconds to cook the turmeric. Add the frozen coconut and continue stir-frying until it thaws and the kale is tender. Taste and season with lemon juice and adjust the salt, if necessary. It's ready to serve.

Serves 2–3

Pumpkin is used quite a lot in Sri Lankan cooking, and there are many varieties available. Elsewhere, your choice of pumpkin might be more limited, so use yellow or orange pumpkin or butternut squash. I particularly like to serve this alongside hoppers (page 286).

Pumpkin & Toasted Coconut Curry
wattaka kalu pol

2 tablespoons coconut oil
¼ teaspoon cumin seeds
¼ teaspoon fennel seeds
¼ teaspoon black mustard seeds
10 fresh or dried curry leaves
2 garlic cloves, finely chopped
1 long, thin green chilli, thinly sliced
1 onion, thinly sliced
600g yellow or orange pumpkin or butternut squash, peeled, deseeded and cut into 2.5cm cubes
400ml coconut milk
2 teaspoons Sri Lankan Toasted Curry Powder (page 272)
½ teaspoon ground turmeric
4 tablespoons desiccated coconut, toasted, or 2 tablespoons *kerisik* (see Atul's tip, below)
sea salt

Heat a wok over a medium-high heat. Add the coconut oil and swirl it around until it melts. Add the cumin seeds, fennel seeds and mustard seeds, and stir until they crackle and pop. Add the curry leaves, garlic, green chilli and onion, and fry, stirring often, until the onion is lightly browned. This can take up to 10 minutes, so watch closely that it doesn't catch on the bottom of the pan and burn.

Add the pumpkin cubes and stir for 3–4 minutes to heat through. Stir in the coconut milk and bring to the boil, then reduce the heat and simmer, uncovered, for 10–15 minutes, stirring occasionally, until the pumpkin is tender. Stir in the curry powder, turmeric and salt to taste, and continue simmering for 2–3 minutes for the spices to cook and blend into the coconut milk.

Stir in the toasted coconut and simmer for a further 5 minutes, stirring frequently to prevent the curry from sticking to the bottom of the wok. Taste and adjust the salt, if necessary. It's ready to serve.

● atul's tip

Sri Lankans often make their own toasted coconut paste, and you can find numerous recipes online. I suggest you buy *kerisik* from an Asian grocer, or, simply use lightly toasted desiccated coconut.

Lentils are a crowd-pleasing ingredient all over the Indian subcontinent, and that certainly holds true in Sri Lanka, where cooks are very creative with their lentil preparations. Lentils are packed with nutrients and are a must for most meals, especially vegetarian ones. This recipe is a typical one on the domestic level, and pleases every palate it touches. You can also include carrots, pumpkin, cucumber, beans or just about any vegetable you like with the lentils in this curry.

Red Lentil Curry with Spinach
kirai payaru

250g split red lentils (*masoor daal*), rinsed and soaked for 20 minutes in cold water to cover
600ml water
3 tablespoons coconut or sunflower oil
10 fresh or dried curry leaves
4 garlic cloves, thinly sliced
1 dried red chilli
1 teaspoon black mustard seeds
1 large onion, thinly sliced
1 teaspoon Sri Lankan Toasted Curry Powder (page 272)
½ teaspoon ground turmeric
300g baby spinach leaves, rinsed and shaken dry
300ml coconut milk
sea salt
fried curry leaves, to garnish, optional

Drain the lentils. Put them, the 600ml water and a pinch of salt in a deep saucepan over a high heat and bring to the boil. Reduce the heat to medium and leave the lentils to simmer for 15 minutes, or until tender. Drain well and return to the saucepan. Cover to keep hot and set aside.

Meanwhile, heat a wok over a medium-high heat. Add the coconut oil and swirl it around as it melts. Add the curry leaves, garlic, chilli and mustard seeds, and stir-fry until the mustard seeds pop. Watch that the garlic doesn't burn. Reduce the heat slightly, add the onion and continue stir-frying until it turns light brown.

Add the curry powder and turmeric and continue stirring for 30 seconds. Stir in the spinach leaves and as they wilt, add the coconut milk and cooked lentils. Make sure everything is mixed together and simmering, then taste and adjust the salt, if necessary, and garnish with fried curry leaves, if using. It's ready to serve.

This street food curry is one of my favourites from Sri Lanka. I can eat this rich, hot and satisfying dish all day long. It is traditionally made with a local flatbread called *godhambara roti*, but parathas (page 289) or tortillas work just as well.

Vegetable Curry with Bread
kottu roti

5 parathas or soft flour tortillas
2 tablespoons vegetable oil
1 onion, sliced
3 garlic cloves, chopped
2 fat green chillies, sliced
1.5cm piece of fresh ginger, peeled and finely chopped
150g cabbage, cored and shredded
1 large green pepper, cored, deseeded and cut into strips
½ teaspoon red chilli powder
150g carrots, peeled and grated
4 spring onions, shredded
3 eggs, beaten
sea salt
chopped fresh coriander leaves, to garnish

For the Sri Lankan Curry Sauce
200ml vegetable stock
1 tablespoon Sri Lankan Toasted Curry Powder (page 272)
1 teaspoon English mustard powder
½ teaspoon ground cinnamon
¼ teaspoon red chilli powder
¼ teaspoon freshly ground black pepper
2 tablespoons chopped coriander leaves
2 tablespoons freshly squeezed lemon juice

Heat a large, dry non-stick frying pan over a medium heat. Cook each paratha for 3–5 minutes, turning over every 30 seconds or so, gently applying pressure to ensure even cooking, until golden. If using tortillas, cook each one for 1–2 minutes. Wrap the breads in foil and cover in a tea towel to keep warm while you cook the rest of the recipe.

To make the curry sauce, place all the ingredients, except the coriander leaves and lemon juice, in a small saucepan over a high heat and bring to the boil, stirring. Lower the heat and simmer for 10 minutes, uncovered, and then add the chopped coriander and lemon juice. Set aside.

Meanwhile, heat a wok over a high heat. Add the oil and swirl it around. Add the onion and stir-fry until it is translucent. Add the garlic, green chillies and ginger, and continue stir-frying until the onion is lightly browned. Watch closely so the garlic doesn't burn. Add the cabbage and green pepper and stir-fry for a further 2 minutes.

Stir in the chilli powder and the prepared sauce, and continue stirring until the cabbage and green pepper are softened. Add the carrots, spring onions and eggs with salt to taste, stirring constantly. When the eggs are scrambled, shred the parathas or tortillas into the curry and continue stirring until the pieces are coated with spices and curry sauce. Sprinkle with coriander leaves and serve.

This is a pretty unusual recipe. Throughout the Indian subcontinent fresh coconut palm heart is often used in curries, but in the UK palm hearts are not that easy to find. I found canned palm hearts in a local supermarket, however, and they have turned out to be a pretty good substitute. The other ingredients in this recipe you might not be familiar with are pandan leaves and bilimbi, a sour fruit. If you can't find either at a good Asian food shop, substitute a few drops of pandan essence for the former and lime juice for the latter. I serve this with freshly boiled basmati rice (page 283).

Colombo Palm Heart Curry
kithul bada kari

2 tablespoons coconut oil
1 teaspoon black mustard seeds
2 red onions, chopped
10–12 fresh or dried curry leaves
3 long, thin green chillies, thinly sliced
1 small fresh pandan leaf, or 2 drops of edible pandan essence to be added after the cooking is finished
4 bilimbi, sliced, or 1 tablespoon lime juice to be added after the cooking is finished
2 teaspoons Sri Lankan Toasted Curry Powder (page 272)
1 teaspoon ground turmeric
½ teaspoon ground black pepper
2 x 410g cans palm hearts, drained and sliced
400ml coconut milk
sea salt

Heat a wok over a high heat. Add the coconut oil and swirl it around until it melts. Add the mustard seeds and stir until they pop. Add the red onions, curry leaves, green chillies and pandan leaf, if using, and stir until the onion begins to soften.

Stir in the bilimbi, if using, curry powder, turmeric and black pepper, and stir for 30 seconds to cook the spices.

Stir in the palm hearts, coconut milk and a pinch of salt to taste. Reduce the heat a little and leave to simmer for 10–12 minutes until slightly reduced. Add the pandan essence and lime juice, if using. Serve at once.

Egg curries are common throughout India, but this version is so different from the ones I most often cook and eat. It's the curry powder and pandan leaf that make this recipe stand out. I love eating this curry with hoppers (page 286), or even dosas (rice pancakes), but for a simpler meal, plain boiled basmati rice (page 283) works just as well.

Sri Lankan Egg Curry
muttai kulamba

6 eggs
3 tablespoons vegetable oil
2 long, thin green chillies, thinly sliced
1 onion, thinly sliced
1 tomato, chopped
½ pandan leaf, finely chopped, or one drop edible pandan essence
2.5cm piece of cinnamon bark
1 teaspoon Sri Lankan Toasted Curry Powder (page 272)
½ teaspoon ground turmeric
¼ teaspoon red chilli powder
¼ teaspoon prepared English mustard
100ml water
200ml coconut milk
sea salt
sorrel leaves, to garnish

First, hard-boil the eggs. Bring a large saucepan of water to the boil. Carefully lower the eggs into the water and add a large pinch of salt. Be careful the water doesn't splash as you add the eggs. Cover the pan and return the water to the boil, then turn the heat to a low boil so bubbles just break the surface. Leave the eggs to cook for 9 minutes. Drain the eggs and then put them under running cold water to stop the cooking. Shell the eggs.

Heat 2 tablespoons of the oil in a large saucepan over a medium heat. Add the eggs and fry for about 10 minutes to let them colour and shrivel a bit. Remove the eggs from the pan, cut in half and set aside on a plate.

Add the remaining tablespoon of oil to the pan, still over a medium heat. Add all the remaining ingredients, except the eggs, water and coconut milk, and fry, stirring often, for 3–4 minutes to cook the spices and blend the flavours. Stir in the water, lower the heat and leave to simmer for 5 minutes. Add the eggs and coconut milk and continue simmering, uncovered, until the sauce thickens slightly. Season with salt to taste, garnish and it's ready to serve.

Soya mince has been used in my kitchens for a long time as a popular meat alternative. When I was growing up in India, soya nuggets and mince were novelty ingredients, but today they are positively mainstream. (If you've never tried soya mince before, you'll find it in supermarkets.) There isn't much flavour in soya mince, but it is nutritious, so I've paired it with some stronger flavours for a vegan twist on this Indian restaurant favourite. Here I'm finishing the dish with fresh ginger, but another twist would be to add fresh lemon juice just before serving and too garnish with very thinly sliced red onions.

Soya Mince & Pea Curry

soya keema mutter

150g dried soya mince, or 500g rehydrated soya mince
2 tablespoons vegetable oil
2.5cm piece of cinnamon bark
2 cloves
2 green cardamom pods, bruised
1 dried bay leaf
1 teaspoon cumin seeds
2 onions, finely chopped
2 teaspoons Ginger-Garlic Paste (page 281)
2 tomatoes, chopped
1 tablespoon ground coriander
1 teaspoon garam masala
1 teaspoon ground turmeric
½ teaspoon mild red chilli powder
¼ teaspoon ground black pepper
150g frozen peas
sea salt
1 tablespoon chopped coriander leaves, to garnish
1.5cm piece of fresh ginger, peeled and finely chopped, to garnish

If using dried soya mince, soak the mince in freshly boiled water to cover for 15 minutes, or until tender and spongy. Drain and rinse it under running cold water, then leave it to sit in the sieve to let the excess water drain away.

Heat the oil in a large wok or frying pan over a medium-high heat. Add the cinnamon, cloves, cardamom pods, bay leaf and cumin seeds, and stir until the seeds crackle. Add the onions and fry, stirring often, until they turn light brown. This can take up to 10 minutes, so watch closely so they don't catch and burn.

Reduce the heat to medium. Add the ginger-garlic paste and continue stirring until the paste looks caramelised. Add the tomatoes and cook, still over a medium heat, stirring occasionally, until the tomatoes break down. Add the ground coriander, garam masala, turmeric, chilli powder, black pepper and salt to taste, and continue stirring for a further 5 minutes, or until the tomatoes are completely broken down. Make sure the ground spices get cooked at this stage.

Add the soya mince and stir for 5 minutes, or until well combined with the tomato mixture and heated through. Add the peas and continue cooking for a further 5 minutes, or until the peas are cooked through and hot. Taste and adjust the salt, if necessary. Garnish with the coriander leaves and fresh ginger just before serving.

● variation: soya keema pie

I use this same mixture to make a meat-free pie for family suppers. Preheat the oven to 190°C/Fan 170°C/Gas 5. Spoon the mixture into an ovenproof serving dish, then all you need is a good potato mash to cover. Place on a baking tray and cook in the oven for 25–30 minutes until the filling is bubbling and the mash turns golden, then it's ready to serve. This is a Tuesday-night favourite in the Kochhar home.

Eggs play a major role in gastronomy across the Indian subcontinent. Sri Lankan cooking has had huge European influences from the Dutch, Portuguese, French and British, so, not surprisingly, the use of eggs in baking and for breakfast is quite common. Sri Lankans' spice instincts propel them to use eggs in curries as well. This dish is an interesting one – an omelette made into a curry. Over the years I have had the pleasure of having many Sri Lankan chefs go through my kitchens, and I've always been interested in watching them cook with spices, as they all had a very different approach from mine. This is a recipe I've developed after years of watching and learning. I serve this with freshly boiled basmati rice (page 283) or dosas (rice pancakes).

Omelette Curry

6 large eggs
2 tomatoes, finely chopped
1 large red onion, finely chopped
1 tablespoon chopped
   green chillies
1 tablespoon rapeseed oil
sea salt

For the curry sauce
1 tablespoon coconut oil
½ teaspoon fenugreek seeds
½ teaspoon black mustard seeds
¼ teaspoon fennel seeds
12–15 fresh or dried curry leaves
2.5cm piece of cinnamon bark
1 tablespoon Sri Lankan Toasted
   Curry Powder (page 272)
1 teaspoon red chilli powder
½ teaspoon ground turmeric
400ml coconut milk
100ml water
sea salt

First, make the omelette. Crack the eggs into a large bowl and whisk in the tomatoes, red onion and green chillies with a pinch of salt.

Heat oil in a large frying pan, ideally non-stick, over a medium-high heat. Add the egg mixture, swirling it around to cover the bottom, then cook for about 2 minutes until the eggs are set and lightly coloured underneath. Carefully turn the omelette over and cook on the other side for 2 minutes, or until lightly coloured. Transfer to a chopping board and leave to rest while you make the curry sauce. Don't worry if the omelette breaks up slightly.

To make the curry sauce, first wash and dry the pan. Melt the coconut oil in the pan over a medium heat. Add the fenugreek seeds, mustard seeds and fennel seeds, and stir-fry until the spices turn darker and pop. Add the curry leaves and continue stirring for a minute, then add the cinnamon bark, curry powder, chilli powder and ground turmeric, and fry, stirring, for 30 seconds to cook the ground spices and until the mixture is fragrant. Add the coconut milk, water and salt to taste, and bring to the boil. Reduce the heat and simmer, uncovered, for 7–8 minutes to reduce slightly.

Meanwhile, cut the omelette into 3cm squares. Gently stir the omelette squares into the sauce and simmer to reheat. Taste and adjust the salt, if necessary. It's ready to serve.

Serves 5 as a sharing dish

Sindh is in Pakistan, and there is a large community of Sindhi Hindus, who are predominantly vegetarians. These spicy aubergine slices are an example of the Sindhi food I think is very special. *Tariyal* means 'fried', so these are spicy and fried – what else do you need? Choose medium-sized aubergines for this recipes as large ones can be difficult to fry. I particularly like these with mint raita (page 292) or yogurt & mustard seed chutney (page 293), but any chutney will work.

Sindhi Aubergine Slices
tariyal vanga

2 aubergines, cut crossways into 2cm thick slices
vegetable oil for deep-frying
sea salt
your favourite chutney (page 293), to serve
pea shoots, to garnish, optional

For the spice mixture
1 tablespoon ground coriander
1 teaspoon ground toasted cumin seeds (page 270)
1 teaspoon mango powder (*amchur*)
½ teaspoon ground turmeric
¼ teaspoon red chilli powder
¼ teaspoon Sindhi Garam Masala (page 272) or ordinary garam masala

Rub the aubergine slices with salt, then set aside for 30 minutes to draw out extra moisture. Rinse and pat dry with kitchen paper, then use the tip of a sharp knife to lightly slash the top of each slice.

Meanwhile, mix all the ground spices for the spice mixture together with salt to taste in a small bowl, then set aside. Preheat the oven to 180°C/Fan 160°C/Gas 4 and line a large baking tray with 2 layers of kitchen paper.

Heat enough vegetable oil for deep-frying in a deep-fat fryer or heavy-based saucepan until it reaches 190°C. Add as many aubergine slices as will fit without overcrowding the pan and deep-fry until golden brown on both sides. Transfer the slices to the baking tray to drain. Cook in batches, if necessary, reheating the oil to the correct temperature between batches.

Transfer the slices to another baking tray in a single layer and generously sprinkle with the spice mixture. Place the tray in the oven and roast for 7–10 minutes until the spices form a crust on each slice. Serve hot with chutney on the side.

Serves 4 as a sharing dish

Lotus roots from the Indian subcontinent are thinner and smaller than those found in East Asia. If you are using the larger variety, use half the quantity. You can also use canned lotus roots when fresh or frozen are not available. I would serve this with another curry and chapatis (page 288) or basmati rice (page 283).

Lotus Root & Potato Curry
beeh patata ain degh

8 lotus roots, peeled, washed and cut widthways into 1cm slices, or 2 x 400g cans lotus roots, drained
1 teaspoon ghee
2 tablespoons rapeseed oil
a pinch of asafoetida
2 teaspoons cumin seeds
2 onions, finely chopped
2 long, thin green chillies, chopped
2 large potatoes, scrubbed and cut into 2cm wedges with skin on
1 small aubergine, cut into 2cm cubes
3cm piece of fresh ginger, peeled and chopped
4 teaspoons ground coriander
1 teaspoon ground cumin
1 teaspoon Sindhi Garam Masala (page 272), or ordinary garam masala
1 teaspoon ground turmeric
100g fresh or frozen peas
2 tomatoes, chopped
400ml water
sea salt
1 tablespoon lemon juice
chopped coriander leaves or celery cress, to garnish

If using fresh lotus roots, put the slices in a saucepan of water, bring to the boil and boil for 2–3 minutes until tender-crisp. Drain well and rinse with cold water to stop the cooking, then set aside.

Heat a large wok that can be covered over a medium-high heat. Add the ghee and rapeseed oil, and swirl it around. Add the asafoetida and stir until it foams and subsides. Add the cumin seeds and stir-fry until they crackle. Add the onions and continue stir-frying until they are lightly browned. Add the green chillies, potatoes, aubergine, ginger, ground coriander, ground cumin, garam masala and turmeric, and continue stirring for 30 seconds to cook the ground spices. Watch closely so they don't catch and burn.

Add the lotus roots, peas and tomatoes to the wok, and continue stir-frying until the tomatoes soften. Stir in the water with salt to taste and bring to the boil. Reduce the heat and simmer, partially covered, for 15 minutes, turning the potatoes occasionally, or until they are tender. Add a small amount of extra water, if necessary, so the potatoes don't stick.

Remove the pan from heat, stir in the lemon juice, taste and adjust the salt, if necessary. Sprinkle with coriander leaves or celery cress and serve.

When I was growing up, friends' mothers often cooked this for Diwali, the traditional festival of lights. This is a vegan version, but you can add pan-fried paneer for a vegetarian option. Serve with basmati rice (page 283) and parathas (page 289).

Pakistani Mixed Vegetable Curry
chiti kuni

2 floury potatoes, such as King Edwards, peeled
3 onions, halved
200g green beans, topped and tailed
2 carrots, peeled and chopped
½ cauliflower, cut into florets
5cm piece of fresh ginger, peeled and chopped
8 garlic cloves
2 long, thin green chillies, halved
14 okra pods, stem ends removed and the pods halved lengthwise
1 tablespoon chickpea flour (*besan*)
pinch of red chilli powder
2 teaspoons ground turmeric, plus an extra pinch
sunflower oil
4 teaspoons ground coriander
250ml passata
100g fresh fenugreek leaves, chopped and rinsed
100g spinach leaves, chopped and rinsed
1 courgette, chopped
sea salt

Put the potatoes in a large saucepan of salted water over a high heat. Bring to the boil and simmer for 20–25 minutes until they are tender. Drain, rinse under cold running water and drain well again. Cut the potatoes into bite-sized pieces and set aside.

Put the onions in a large saucepan with water to cover and bring to the boil. Reduce the heat and simmer for 20 minutes, until they are tender and a knife slides in easily. Strain the onions, reserving the water. Put the onions in a blender or food processor and blend until a purée forms. Set aside.

Return the onion cooking water to the pan with a large pinch of salt and bring to the boil. One at a time, add the green beans, carrot, and cauliflower, and cook until tender. As each vegetable becomes tender, remove with a slotted spoon and transfer to a colander. Place under running cold water to stop the cooking, then set aside.

Meanwhile, put the ginger, garlic and green chillies in a spice blender, coffee grinder or small food processor, and grind until a paste forms. Set aside.

Toss the okra pods with the chickpea flour, chilli powder, turmeric and salt to taste. Heat about a 0.5cm layer of oil in a large frying pan over a medium-high heat. Add as many okra halves as will fit and fry, turning occasionally, until crisp on both sides. Transfer to a plate lined with kitchen paper to drain, then continue until all are cooked.

Heat 2 tablespoons sunflower oil in a large saucepan with a lid over a medium heat. Add the onion purée, standing well back because it will splutter. Fry, stirring frequently and adding water as necessary, until the paste is light mahogany brown (see Atul's tip, below).

Add the ginger-garlic-chilli paste and continue stirring for 1 minute to cook out the rawness. Stir in the ground coriander and continue frying for 30 seconds. Add a little water, if necessary. The mixture should be a bit darker and smell wonderful at this point.

Stir in the passata with salt to taste and continue stirring. Stir in the fenugreek leaves and spinach leaves, cover the pan and leave to simmer for 5–7 minutes, stirring occasionally, until the leaves wilt into the sauce. The fenugreek leaves will taste bitter if not completely cooked at this point.

Add the green beans, carrots, potatoes and courgette, and stir together until they are all coated with the sauce. Add the cauliflower florets and enough water so all the vegetables are covered. Set aside a few okra slices for garnish, then stir the remainder into the curry and bring to the boil. Lower the heat and simmer, uncovered, until the vegetables are tender and the flavours blended. Taste and adjust the salt, garnish and serve.

● atul's tip

When I start frying the onion purée I put a jug of water near the hob, because the purée has a tendency to catch on the bottom of the pan. If this happens, add a couple of tablespoons water and stir to incorporate. The caramelisation from the browning process adds flavour, but watch closely to prevent burning. There is no way to disguise the burnt flavour and you will have to start again.

I grew up eating this vegetable stew in the homes of my many Sindhi friends. This is a good one-pot meal that is prepared year-round, and traditionally made with dried vegetables during the winter months. Serve this with brown basmati rice (page 283) and the bread of your choice; I would opt for naans (page 287).

Sindhi Vegetable Curry
said bhaji

200g dried split brown chickpeas (*channa daal* or Bengal gram), rinsed and soaked in cold water to cover for 20 minutes
1 litre water
500g spinach leaves, rinsed
2 long, thin green chillies, stem ends removed, but left whole
2 tomatoes, chopped
1 large carrot, peeled and chopped
1 onion, chopped
1 floury potato, such as King Edward, peeled and chopped
2.5cm piece of fresh ginger, peeled and chopped
1 tablespoon ground coriander
1 teaspoon Sindhi Garam Masala (page 272), or to taste
1 teaspoon ground turmeric
sea salt and freshly ground black pepper

For the tarka
2 tablespoons sunflower oil
2 garlic cloves, chopped
1 teaspoon cumin seeds

Drain the split chickpeas. Put them in a large saucepan with a lid, add the water and bring to the boil, skimming the surface, as necessary. Add the spinach, green chillies, tomatoes, carrot, onion, potato, ginger, ground coriander, garam masala, turmeric and salt to taste, and give everything a good stir. Cover the pan, return to the boil and simmer for 20 minutes, or until the chickpeas are very tender. You should be able to squeeze them between your fingers.

Uncover the pan and use a potato masher to mash the chickpeas and vegetables together, but not so much that they lose all their texture. Season with more garam masala, salt and/or pepper to taste, then re-cover the pan and simmer for a further 10 minutes. If the gravy is too liquid for you, uncover the pan and just keep simmering until you have a consistency you like.

Just before serving, prepare the tarka. Heat the oil in a small pan over a high heat. Add the garlic and cumin seeds and fry until the garlic turns light brown and the cumin crackles. Watch closely so the garlic doesn't burn. Immediately tip the oil and flavourings into the chickpeas – stand back, because they will splutter. If you have any seeds left in the small pan, add a little of the lentil mixture and stir around to scrape any browned bits from the base, then add to the larger pan. Stir everything together, taste and adjust the seasoning before serving.

This is a healthy and delicious everyday dal. The bold flavour comes from cumin and fenugreek seeds that are added just before serving. Whenever I discuss this recipe with Sindhi friends, without fail each and every one of them will insist that their grandparents cooked the best version of this traditional recipe, and that it was even better than their mother's!

Sour Lentil Dal
sindhi khatti daal

200g split yellow peas (*toor daal* or split pigeon peas), rinsed and soaked in cold water to cover for 20 minutes
750ml water
½ teaspoon red chilli powder
½ teaspoon ground turmeric
1.5cm piece of fresh ginger, peeled and chopped
10 fresh or dried curry leaves
1 long, thin green chilli, cut in half
1 tomato, chopped
1 tablespoon tamarind extract (see Atul's tip, page 167)
1 tablespoon chopped coriander leaves
sea salt

For the tarka
2 tablespoons sunflower oil
1½ teaspoons cumin seeds
1 teaspoon fenugreek seeds

Drain the split yellow peas and transfer them to a saucepan with the water. Stir in the chilli powder, turmeric and ½ teaspoon salt. Bring to the boil, skimming the surface, as necessary, then simmer for 20 minutes, or until the split peas are very tender. Use the back of your spoon to lightly mash some of the split peas, leaving most whole.

Stir in the ginger, curry leaves, green chilli and tomato, then simmer, uncovered and stirring often, for about 10 minutes until the tomatoes break down. Add a splash of water if the mixture starts sticking to the bottom of the pan.

Add the tamarind extract. Don't be tempted to add the tamarind earlier, as it stops the lentils becoming tender.

Just before serving, prepare the tarka. Heat the oil in a small pan over a high heat. Add the cumin and fenugreek seeds and fry until the cumin seeds crackle and the fenugreek seeds turn darker. Immediately tip the oil and seeds into the split peas – stand back, because they will splutter. If you have any seeds left in the small pan, add a little of the lentil mixture and stir around to remove the browned bits, then add to the larger pan. Stir in the coriander leaves and serve.

Versions of this simple curry are prepared throughout the entire Indian subcontinent, from Pakistan to Sri Lanka, and this is my contribution. Guwar beans, commonly known as cluster beans, are the traditional ingredient, but more readily available green beans make an excellent substitute. Potatoes are also often added, as are onion pakoras. I've given you a vegan recipe here, with a vegetarian option of adding yogurt, a traditional Punjabi ingredient. I think this is excellent served with fresh basmati rice (page 283) and Mixed Vegetable Curry (page 218) or Afghani Kidney Bean Curry (page 228).

Okra & Bean Curry
sindhi kadhi

4 tablespoons sunflower oil
¼ teaspoon asafoetida
1 teaspoon cumin seeds
½ teaspoon fenugreek seeds
4 tablespoons chickpea (*besan*) flour
3 tablespoons Greek yogurt, optional
800ml water
1.5cm piece fresh ginger, peeled and crushed
10 fresh or dried curry leaves
2 long, thin green chillies, stem ends removed, but left whole
1 tablespoon ground coriander
1 teaspoon red chilli powder
1 teaspoon ground turmeric
200g green beans, topped and tailed, but left whole
12 okra pods, stem ends removed and pods chopped
3 tablespoons tamarind extract (see Atul's tip, page 167)
sea salt
chopped coriander leaves, to garnish

Heat the oil in a large saucepan over a medium-high heat. Add the asafoetida and stir until it foams and subsides. Even though this is such a small amount, it really gives a distinctive character to this particular dish. Add the cumin seeds and fenugreek seeds and stir until the cumin seeds crackle and the fenugreek seeds darken, which will happen very quickly. These are the flavour builders in this recipe.

Add the chickpea flour and continue stirring until it absorbs the oil and turns crumbly and light brown.

If using the yogurt, whisk it together with the water, then add to the pan and whisk constantly as it comes to the boil to prevent it splitting. If not using the yogurt, just add the water and bring to the boil, stirring. Reduce the heat and add the ginger, curry leaves, green chillies, ground coriander, chilli powder, turmeric and a pinch of salt to taste. Return to the boil and whisk until the gravy is smooth and starting to thicken.

Reduce the heat again, stir in the green beans, okra and tamarind, and leave to simmer, uncovered, for 15 minutes, or until the vegetables are tender. Taste and adjust the salt, if necessary. Garnish and serve.

Makes 16

These filled wonton wrappers can be steamed or boiled, but I prefer the simple technique I use here of browning them first and then steam-frying them in the same pan. I learned this technique from my friend David Thompson, the chef and Thai-cooking authority, and I think it gives the cooked pot-stickers a very satisfying texture.

Pot-stickers
subz aushak

16 wonton wrappers (about 100g), 8 x 8cm, thawed if frozen
1 egg, beaten
sunflower oil
sea salt and freshly ground black pepper
chopped coriander leaves, to garnish

For the filling
2 tablespoons sunflower oil
2 garlic cloves, chopped
150g trimmed leeks, halved, thinly sliced and rinsed
2 spring onions, thinly sliced
1 teaspoon ground coriander
¼ teaspoon sweet paprika
50g paneer, grated
1 tablespoon chopped coriander leaves
½ lemon

For the tomato-soya sauce
30g dried soya mince or 125g rehydrated soya mince
2 tablespoons sunflower oil
2 garlic cloves, chopped
1 onion, chopped
2 teaspoons ground coriander

If using dried soya mince in the sauce, soak it in freshly boiled water to cover for 15 minutes, or until tender and spongy. Drain and rinse the mince in running cold water, then leave it to sit in the sieve to let the excess water drain away.

Next, make the filling. Heat the oil in a large frying pan over a medium-high heat. Add the garlic and fry, stirring, for about 30 seconds to flavour the oil – you don't want the garlic to colour. Add the leeks, spring onions, ground coriander, paprika and a pinch of salt, and continue stirring until the leeks soften.

Add the paneer and chopped coriander and season with lemon juice and salt and pepper to taste, stirring until all the ingredients are blended. Set aside to cool.

Working with one wrapper at a time, place about 2 teaspoons of the filling off-centre and fold over to make a triangle. Lightly brush the inside edges with the beaten egg and press to seal. Cover with a tea towel and set aside while you fill all the wrappers and until you are ready to cook them.

To make the tomato-soya sauce, heat the oil in a saucepan over a medium-high heat. Add the garlic and fry, stirring, until it softens. Add the onion with a pinch of salt and continue frying, stirring

1 teaspoon red chilli powder
¼ teaspoon ground cardamom
¼ teaspoon black pepper
400ml passata
125ml water
8 tablespoons chopped
   coriander leaves

For the yogurt sauce
200g full-fat natural yogurt
1 garlic clove, crushed
½ teaspoon dried mint, crushed
½ lemon

occasionally, until it is light brown. Watch closely so nothing burns.

Add the soya mince and stir it into the onion, scraping the bottom of the pan, if necessary. Add the ground coriander, red chilli powder and ground cardamom, and stir for 30 seconds to cook the ground spices. Keep a jug of water by the hob and add a little, when necessary, to stop the soya mince from catching too much on the bottom of the pan. Stir in the black pepper and salt to taste, but remember the onion was salted.

Stir in the passata and water, using the water to get all the passata out of the measuring jug – you don't want to waste any. Bring to the boil, then reduce the heat and leave to simmer, uncovered and stirring occasionally, for about 15 minutes.

Meanwhile, make the yogurt sauce. Put the yogurt in a bowl and stir in the crushed garlic, dried mint and salt to taste. Squeeze in lemon juice to taste, making sure you pick out any pips. Stir again, then set aside until required.

When you are ready to cook the pot-stickers, heat a thin layer of oil in 1 or 2 large frying pans with lids, ideally non-stick, over a medium-high heat. Add as many pot-stickers as will fit in a single layer and fry just until they turn golden brown on the bottom. Carefully turn them over and continue to colour the other side. Reduce the heat, add a splash of water and immediately cover the pans. The water will be sizzling and bubbling in the pan, which softens the wrappers. Cook in batches and keep hot, if you don't have 2 pans with lids.

When you're ready to serve, return the tomato sauce to the boil. Stir in the coriander, taste and adjust the salt, if necessary. Divide the wontons among plates and top each portion with a couple of spoonfuls of the tomato-soya sauce. Add a spoonful of the yogurt sauce to each plate, garnish with coriander leaves and serve.

A friend gave this recipe to me, and I think it illustrates the culinary links Afghanistan has with neighbouring Pakistan and Iran. The recipe calls for vegetable stock or water and I recommend using water if your stock has a strong herb flavour, which you don't want in this recipe. If you'd rather make this with dried beans cooked in a pressure cooker, as we do in the Kochhar household, start with 200g dried beans. I then add them to the pan with their cooking liquid.

Kidney Bean Curry
qorma e lubya

4 tablespoons sunflower oil
1 tablespoon coriander seeds
1 teaspoon cumin seeds
1 can (400g) chopped tomatoes, or 400g fresh tomatoes, chopped
½ teaspoon dried mint
1 onion, chopped
4 garlic cloves, chopped
2 x 400g cans red kidney beans
125ml vegetable stock, ideally home-made (page 282), or water
1 teaspoon freshly ground black pepper
sea salt
pea shoots or chopped coriander leaves, to garnish

Heat 2 tablespoons of the oil in a large saucepan over a medium-high heat. Add the coriander seeds and cumin seeds and fry, stirring, until the coriander seeds turn a shade darker and the cumin seeds crackle. Stir in the tomatoes (be careful as the oil will splatter), dried mint and 1 teaspoon salt, or to taste, and bring to the boil, using a spoon to break up the tomatoes.

Tip the mixture into a blender or food processor and blend until smooth. Set aside.

Meanwhile, heat the remaining 2 tablespoon oil in the washed and dried pan over a medium-high heat. Add the onion with a pinch of salt and fry, stirring occasionally, until it is softened. Add the garlic and continue frying, stirring frequently, until the onions are light brown. Watch closely so the garlic does not catch and burn.

Stir in the kidney beans with the liquid from the cans, the puréed tomato mixture, vegetable stock and the black pepper. Bring to the boil, then reduce the heat and simmer, uncovered, for 30–40 minutes, stirring occasionally. Taste and adjust the salt, if necessary. Garnish with coriander and serve.

Makes 8

Kabul is said to be home to the best *balonis*, a popular of street food; they remind me of Italian calzones. There are almost infinite variations possible for the filling, but I've kept it simple with sautéed leeks, a vegetable used a great deal in Afghani cooking. In this recipe I'm using sunflower oil so it remains vegan, but if you are vegetarian and want real richness, use butter or ghee.

Leek-stuffed Breads
baloni

200g plain white flour
150g chapati (*atta*) flour or plain wholemeal flour, plus extra for dusting
1 tablespoon sunflower oil, plus a little extra for cooking
200–220ml water
sea salt and freshly ground black pepper

For the filling
3 tablespoons sunflower oil
4 trimmed leeks, about 500g, thinly sliced
2 long, thin green chillies, thinly sliced
3 spring onions, trimmed and finely chopped
5 tablespoons coriander leaves, finely chopped
1 teaspoon pomegranate seed powder, or use sumac or lemon juice

To make the dough, put the plain white and chapati flours in a large bowl with a pinch each of salt and black pepper. Make a well in the centre and add the oil, then gradually pour in the water and use your fingers to mix together to form a semi-soft dough, working in the flour from the side. When the dough is the correct consistency, all the flour will be incorporated. Knead lightly into a ball, then cover with a damp tea towel and set aside for 30 minutes.

Meanwhile, make the filling. Heat the oil in a large frying pan over a medium-high heat. Add the leeks, green chillies and a pinch each of salt and black pepper, and fry, stirring often, for 10–15 minutes until the leeks are tender and reduced in volume.

Turn off the heat and stir in the spring onions, coriander leaves and pomegranate seed powder. Taste and adjust the salt, if necessary. Set aside to cool while you roll out the dough.

Divide the dough into 8 equal portions. Working with one piece at a time, place it on a very lightly floured surface, roll out into a 23cm round, dusting with flour, as necessary, then pat the dough back and forth between your hands to remove the excess flour. Place one-eighth of the filling on one side of the dough circle, leaving a 2.5cm border. Brush the edge of the dough all round with water, then bring the uncovered half over the filling and press the edges firmly together to seal. Continue until all the breads are assembled.

Heat 1 or 2 large, ideally non-stick, *tawas* or frying pans over a high heat. Add as many stuffed breads as will fit in a single layer and dry-fry until they are speckled light brown. Carefully flip them over and repeat, pressing down gently with a spatula, especially around the edge. You don't want to leave any dough raw, but you also want to be careful not to burn them.

Traditionally, these are cooked in a thick layer of oil, which ensures the folded edge fries and is cooked. However, I want to keep the amount of oil to a minimum so use your spatula and fingers to hold the bread upright, with the folded edge against the pan for 30 seconds–1 minute until the dough around the edges is cooked.

When the dough is speckled with brown on both sides, lightly brush the top with oil and flip it over. Cook for about 30 seconds, then repeat on the other side, pressing down with the spatula along the sealed edge to make sure the dough is cooked through.

These are best served as soon as they come off the pan, but if you want to cook then all first, wrap them in a tea towel to keep warm and. Cut each one into quarters for eating with your fingers.

The cinnamon and fennel flavour combination works really well with the tart kick from the unripe mango in this simple curry. As an Indian, I'm used to flavouring the oil with whole spices before adding other ingredients, but this recipe is typical of Maldivian cooking in that the spices, onion and garlic are cooked together. If you've not prepared a green mango before, you'll find the seed is surrounded with a thin membrane that can be scraped away with a small spoon before cooking.

Green Mango Curry
anbu kari

2 tablespoons sunflower oil
3cm piece of cinnamon bark
2.5cm piece of fresh ginger, peeled and cut into julienne strips
10 fresh or dried curry leaves
5 garlic cloves, chopped
3 cloves
2 long, thin green chillies, stem ends removed, but kept whole
1 red onion, chopped
1 teaspoon fennel seeds
1 tablespoon Sri Lankan Toasted Curry Powder (page 272)
1 teaspoon red chilli powder
1 teaspoon ground turmeric
8–10 green mangoes, halved, stoned, inner membrane removed, flesh removed and quartered
250ml water
250ml coconut milk
sea salt

Heat the oil in a large frying pan with a lid over a medium-high heat. Add the cinnamon bark, ginger, curry leaves, garlic, cloves, green chillies, red onion and fennel seeds, and fry, stirring often, until the onion is just beginning to brown.

Stir in the curry powder, chilli powder, turmeric and salt to taste. Add the mangoes and continue stirring for 30 seconds to cook the ground spices and to ensure the mango pieces are well coated. Stir in the water to stop the onion and spices from catching on the bottom of the pan. It should be smelling wonderful at this point.

Bring to the boil, then cover the pan, lower the heat and leave the mangoes to simmer for 20–25 minutes until they are just tender. Stir in the coconut milk and bring to the boil. Reduce the heat and leave to simmer, uncovered, for 5–10 minutes for the flavours to blend and the gravy to thicken. Taste and adjust the salt, if necessary. It's ready to serve.

I have eaten Maldivian food many times and it never fails to remind me of what I eat in Sri Lanka. The combination of cinnamon and cardamom in this mouth-watering recipe smells wonderful as it cooks, and the dish tastes as amazing as it smells. I serve this with freshly boiled basmati rice (page 283), chapatis (page 288) or naans (page 287).

Potato Curry
aluvi kari

4 floury potatoes, such as King Edwards, peeled and halved
2 tablespoons sunflower oil
5 green cardamom pods, bruised
10 fresh or dried curry leaves
1 onion, thinly sliced
3 garlic cloves, chopped
1.5cm piece of fresh ginger, peeled and chopped
1 long, thin green chilli, sliced
250ml coconut milk
6 tablespoons passata, or 3 tablespoons tomato purée
2.5cm piece of cinnamon bark
2 tablespoons Sri Lankan Toasted Curry Powder (page 272)
1 teaspoon ground coriander
1 teaspoon ground turmeric
½ teaspoon red chilli powder
250ml water, or as needed
sea salt

Put the potatoes in a saucepan of salted water to cover and bring to the boil, then boil for 20 minutes or until tender. Drain well, rinse under cold running water and drain well again. When cool enough to handle, cut the potatoes into bite-sized pieces. Set aside.

Meanwhile, heat the oil in another large saucepan over a medium heat. Add the cardamom pods and leave them to sizzle for a few seconds. Add the curry leaves, onion, garlic and ginger, and fry, stirring often, until the onions are translucent.

Add the chilli and continue stirring until the onion turns light brown. If the onion starts catching on the bottom of the pan, stir in a couple tablespoons of water, but watch closely because you don't want a burnt flavour.

Transfer about 1 tablespoon of the onion mixture into the coconut milk and set aside.

Stir the passata, cinnamon bark, curry powder, ground coriander, turmeric and salt to taste into the onions, stirring for 30 seconds to cook the ground spices and form a paste. Stir in the water and leave to gently bubble for a couple minutes.

Pour the coconut milk with the onions into the pan and bring to the boil. Add the chopped potatoes and stir together. When the mixture returns to the boil and the potatoes are hot, taste and adjust the salt, if necessary. It's ready to serve.

atul's tips

This is an infinitely versatile recipe. I've made it with just potatoes in this version, but you can also add green beans and peas, or stir spinach leaves in at the last minute for extra colour.

The reason I boil the potatoes first is because if they were added raw after the coconut milk and passata they would take much longer to cook.

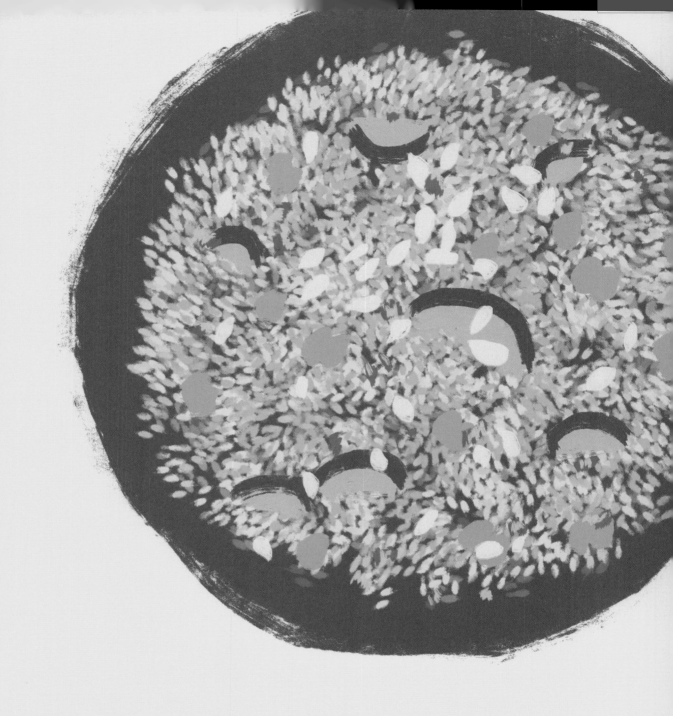

mi

ldle east

This is my vegan version of an Iranian classic, a rich dish with the walnuts and pomegranate flavourings and a hint of cinnamon. You can use vegetable stock if you'd like, but I wanted to keep the flavours of the other ingredients quite pure, which is why I've specified water.

Persian Pumpkin & Chickpea Curry
khoresh fesenjān

½ large pumpkin or butternut
   squash, peeled, deseeded
   and cut into bite-sized cubes,
   about 400g prepared weight
sunflower oil
ground cinnamon
75g walnut halves
2 garlic cloves, finely chopped
1 onion, chopped
7cm piece of cinnamon bark
1 teaspoon ground cumin
1 teaspoon ground turmeric
2 x 400g cans chickpeas, drained
   and rinsed
100ml pomegranate juice
75g pomegranate molasses
½ teaspoon salt
¼ teaspoon ground
   black pepper
freshly grated nutmeg, to taste,
   or a pinch of ground nutmeg
1 unwaxed orange, zested
about 500ml water, as needed
maple syrup, optional
80g pomegranate seeds
salt and ground black pepper
chopped flat-leaf parsley or
   coriander, to garnish

Preheat the oven to 220°C/Fan 200°C/Gas 7. Put the pumpkin cubes on a baking tray lined with baking paper. Drizzle with sunflower oil and lightly dust with ground cinnamon, then shake the tray so all the cubes are well coated. Roast in the oven for 20 minutes or until the pumpkin is tender and the tip of a knife slides through easily.

Meanwhile, heat a frying pan, ideally non-stick, over a medium-high heat. Add the walnuts and toast, stirring often, until lightly browned. Leave to cool, then transfer to a food processor and process until finely ground. Set aside.

Heat 2 tablespoons sunflower oil in a large saucepan over a medium-high heat. Add the garlic and onion and fry, stirring often, until the onions start to soften. Add the cinnamon bark and continue frying, stirring, until the onions are light brown. Stir in the cumin, turmeric and ½ teaspoon ground cinnamon, and stir together for 30 seconds. Add the chickpeas, pomegranate juice, pomegranate molasses, salt, pepper and a good grating of nutmeg. Increase the heat and bring to the boil, stirring.

Add the pumpkin cubes and ground walnuts and return the mixture to the boil, stirring until the stew thickens. Add the orange zest and stir in just enough water to get the thickness you like. Taste and adjust the seasoning, if necessary, and if you think it's too sour add maple syrup to taste. Stir in the pomegranate seeds and garnish with parsley before serving.

I'm merging Iranian and Indian culinary traditions in this recipe. *Khoresh bademjan* is a classic recipe that travelled to the Indian subcontinent with Muslim cooks, where it eventually became *baingan bhurtha*. (Along the way it lost the pomegranate molasses, but acquired typically Indian spices of ground turmeric and red chilli powder.) I think this hybrid version makes a very good starter or a main course if you double all the quantities. Serve with plenty of bread to mop up the generous amount of sauce.

Aubergine Slices with Curried Sauce
khoresh bademjan

1 aubergine, trimmed and cut crossways into six 2cm-thick slices
olive oil
red chilli powder
ground coriander
sea salt and freshly ground black pepper

For the sauce
3 tablespoons olive oil
1 large onion, sliced
250ml passata (see Atul's tip, right)
½ teaspoon ground turmeric
¼ teaspoon red chilli powder
a pinch of saffron powder
1 tablespoon pomegranate molasses
125ml freshly squeezed orange juice
125ml water
freshly squeezed juice of ½ lemon
2 tablespoons sultanas
2 teaspoons melon seeds

Preheat the oven to 220°C/Fan 200°C/Gas 7 and line a baking tray large enough to hold the aubergine slices in a layer with baking paper. Place the slices in the tray and use the tip of a sharp knife to lightly slash the top of each. Drizzle generously with olive oil, then lightly sprinkle with red chilli powder, ground coriander and salt and pepper to taste. Place the tray in the oven and roast for 30–35 minutes until the slices are tender and browned.

Meanwhile, prepare the sauce. Heat the oil in a large frying pan over a medium-high heat. Add the onion and fry, stirring often, until it turns dark golden brown. Watch closely that it doesn't burn. Set aside about 2 tablespoons of the fried onion slices to use as the garnish.

Stir the passata into the onions remaining in the pan, then add the turmeric, red chilli powder, saffron powder and salt and pepper to taste, and continue stirring for 30 seconds to cook the ground spices. Stir in the pomegranate molasses, orange juice, water and lemon juice, and bring to the boil. Leave the sauce to bubble and thicken, then stir in the sultanas and melon seeds and keep warm while you toast the melon seeds for the garnish. I like to

To garnish
1 tablespoon melon seeds
chopped blanched almonds
finely chopped coriander leaves
   or flat-leaf parsley
1 unwaxed orange

serve the sauce warm, not hot. Taste and adjust the salt and pepper, if necessary.

To prepare the garnish, heat a small dry frying pan over a medium-high heat. Add the melon seeds and stir until just toasted. Be careful, because if the pan is too hot, they may splutter.

To serve, divide the aubergine slices among plates. Top the slices with the sauce and reserved onions, then sprinkle over the toasted melon seeds, almonds and coriander or parsley. Grate over the orange zest and it's ready to serve.

---

atul's tip

If you don't have any passata, use 2–3 tablespoons tomato purée mixed into 250ml water.

Thareed is ancient stew mentioned in the Koran, and still popular across the Muslim world, especially for breaking fasts during Ramadan. I've devised this vegan version with tofu for the protein. The distinctive flavouring comes from the cloves in the *bezar* spice powder. Whenever you are served this fragrant and spicy stew in a Middle Eastern country it will be presented on a wafer-thin, crêpe-like bread called *regag*, or *rugag*, which I've included in this recipe.

Vegetable Stew with Regags
thareed

2 tablespoons olive oil

1cm piece of fresh ginger, peeled and chopped

1 garlic clove, chopped

1 onion, chopped

150g aubergine, cut into bite-sized pieces

1 dried lime, punctured all over with a sharp knife

4 tablespoons passata

100g carrots, peeled and sliced

100g courgettes, halved lengthwise and thinly sliced

100g floury potatoes, such as King Edwards, peeled and cut into bite-sized pieces

100g pumpkin or butternut squash, peeled, deseeded and cut into bite-sized pieces

1 tomato, chopped

1 long, thin green chilli, chopped

2 green cardamom pods, lightly crushed

1 tablespoon ground coriander

1 teaspoon red chilli powder

1 teaspoon ground turmeric

¼ teaspoon ground cinnamon

First, make the spice powder. Put the cumin seeds, peppercorns and cloves in a spice grinder or coffee grinder, and grind until a fine powder forms. Add the ground cardamom and ground cinnamon and grind again. Cover to keep it fragrant and set aside.

Heat the olive oil in a large frying pan over a medium-high heat. Add the ginger, garlic and onion and fry, stirring often, until the onions are just starting to brown. It's important to cook out the raw flavours at this point.

Add the aubergine and dried lime and stir around so the aubergine is coated with the onion. Stir in the passata, then add the carrots, courgettes, potatoes, pumpkin, tomato and green chilli with salt to taste, and stir everything together.

Add 1 tablespoon of the spice powder, along with the cardamom pods, ground coriander, chilli powder, turmeric and ground cinnamon, and stir so all the spices are well distributed. (Leftover spice powder can be stored in an airtight container in a dark place to use within 6 months.)

Pour over enough water to just cover the vegetables. Bring to the boil, then reduce the heat and leave to

200g firm tofu, cut into bite-sized chunks
2 tablespoons chopped coriander leaves, plus extra, to garnish
sea salt

For the *bezar* (Emirati spice powder)
1 tablespoon cumin seeds
1 tablespoon black peppercorns
1 teaspoon cloves
1 teaspoon ground cardamom
½ teaspoon ground cinnamon

For the *regags*
140g plain white flour
about 240ml water

simmer, stirring occasionally, until the vegetables are tender.

Meanwhile, make the *regags*. Put the flour and a pinch of salt to taste in a bowl, add the water and whisk together, adding a little extra water, if necessary. The consistency should be of a runny batter rather than a dough. Set aside to rest for 10 minutes.

Heat a large, dry, non-stick frying pan over a high heat. Whisk the batter again. Drop a ladleful of the batter in the centre of the pan, then use the back of the ladle to spread it out as thinly as possible, working in a spiral motion. As the batter cooks and the texture will become crisp and start to bubble (see Atul's tips, below). Tip out of the pan, set aside (keep warm) and continue to make another 3 *regags*.

When the vegetables are tender, stir in the tofu and continue simmering until it is hot. Stir in the coriander leaves, taste and adjust the salt, if necessary. Use the *regags* to line a serving platter or large bowl, then top with the stew. Garnish with more coriander leaves and serve, with any extra *regags* on the side.

atul's tips

Making a *regag* is much like making a French crêpe – it's not difficult, but it does take practice. The first attempt is often destined for the bin. Use a large pan and aim to get the batter as thin as possible. It is cooked through when you can gently slide a spatula under the edge. The batter should be so thin that it only requires cooking on one side – but go ahead and flip if you want. You definitely don't want to be eating raw flour.

Replace the red chilli powder in the stew with paprika if you want a milder flavour.

I absolutely love this recipe as it reminds me of the fragrant pulao rice we make in India. The unique character of this is the *baharat* spice mix. For an extra flourish, or to wow your guests, garnish this with dried rose petals and melon seeds.

Pressed Spicy Rice & Vegetables
machboos

400g white basmati rice, rinsed in running water until the water runs clear, then soaked in fresh water to cover for 30 minutes
3 tablespoons olive oil or ghee
4 garlic cloves, crushed
1 onion, halved and thinly sliced
2 long, thin green chillies, slit lengthways, but left whole
4 green cardamom pods, bruised
4 cloves
1 tablespoon *baharat* (page 276)
1 teaspoon ground turmeric
½ teaspoon cumin seeds
4 tomatoes, finely chopped
1 can (400g) chickpeas, drained and rinsed
3 dried limes, punctured all over with a sharp knife
1 courgette, cut in half lengthways and then cut into 0.5cm half-moon slices
1 red pepper, cored, deseeded and thinly sliced
small handful chopped coriander leaves, plus extra to garnish
small handful chopped parsley leaves, plus extra to garnish
large pinch of saffron threads
1 litre vegetable stock, ideally home-made (page 282)
sea salt and freshly ground black pepper

Drain the basmati rice and set aside.

Heat the oil in a flameproof casserole or a large saucepan with a tight-fitting lid over a medium-high heat. Add the garlic and onion and fry, stirring, until the onion starts to soften. Add the green chillies, cardamom pods, cloves, *baharat*, turmeric, cumin seeds and salt and pepper to taste, and stir together for 30 seconds. Watch closely so the ground spices do not burn. Stir in the tomatoes, cover the pan and leave to cook over a low heat for about 5 minutes until the tomatoes break down.

Add the chickpeas, dried limes, courgette, red pepper, chopped coriander and chopped parsley. Add the drained rice and saffron, stirring until the grains are well coated.

Pour over the vegetable stock and bring to the boil. Cover the casserole, reduce the heat to very low and leave the rice to cook for 10 minutes or until all the water is absorbed and small holes appear on the surface. Re-cover the pan and leave to stand for 5 minutes before serving. Use 2 forks to fluff the rice grains, then taste and adjust the salt and pepper, if necessary. Spoon on to a large platter and garnish with coriander and parsley. It's ready to serve.

This is an ancient, traditional recipe, served with flatbread for scooping up the stew. Fenugreek is a dominant flavour in Yemeni cooking, and *hilbeh* is a common condiment that is often placed on the table for stirring into stews and soups. *Zhoug*, also spelt *z'chug*, gets a fiery kick from the green chillies. *Zhoug* is also stirred into stews and soups across the Middle East, and is often served alongside falafel and flatbreads.

Potato Stew with *Hilbeh & Zhoug*
saltah

4 tablespoons olive oil
2 onions, chopped
1 garlic clove, chopped
⅓ long, thin green chilli, finely chopped
4 floury potatoes, such as King Edwards, peeled and cut into 1cm cubes
2 tomatoes, finely chopped
about 1 litre vegetable stock, ideally home-made (page 282)
sea salt
full-fat natural yogurt, to serve
parsley or coriander leaves, to garnish
flatbreads, to serve

For the *hilbeh* (fenugreek paste)
2 tablespoons fenugreek seeds, soaked in water to just cover for 12 hours or overnight
1 long, thin green chilli, finely chopped
1 garlic clove, finely chopped
1 tomato, finely chopped
1½ tablespoons freshly squeezed lemon juice

Heat the oil in a large saucepan with a lid over a medium-high heat. Add the onions and fry, stirring often, for a couple of minutes until they are beginning to soften. Add the garlic, chilli and a pinch of salt, and continue frying, stirring occasionally, until the onions are translucent.

Add the potatoes and stir them around until coated in the onions. Add the tomatoes with salt to taste and stir together. Pour in enough vegetable stock to just cover the potatoes. Bring to the boil, then reduce the heat and leave to simmer, uncovered, for 30 minutes or until the potatoes are very tender.

Meanwhile, make the *hilbeh*. Transfer the fenugreek seeds and their soaking liquid to a food processor and process until a paste forms, adding a little extra water as necessary. Add the green chilli, garlic, tomato and the lemon juice, and process again to make a smooth, pale paste. Add salt to taste.

To make the *zhoug*, put all the ingredients with salt to taste in a blender or food processor and process until a bright green sauce forms. Taste and adjust the salt, if necessary.

When the potatoes are very tender, use a potato masher to coarsely mash them into the stock. Stir 2 tablespoons of the *hilbeh* into the stew, making

For the *zhoug* (coriander sauce)
50g chopped coriander leaves
2 garlic cloves, peeled
3–4 long, thin green chillies,
    stem ends removed but left
    whole
125ml water
4 tablespoons olive oil
1 teaspoon ground cardamom
1 teaspoon ground coriander
1 teaspoon ground cumin

sure it is well combined. Taste and adjust the salt, if necessary, but remember it contains quite a bit of salt already, then ladle into bowls.

To serve, add a dollop of yogurt to each bowl, with a spoonful of *hilbeh* and *zhoug*. Garnish and serve with the flatbreads.

atul's tips

Zhoug is a great dipping sauce. I also like to use it as a marinade or as a rub for vegetables on the barbecue. You can also serve *zhoug* as a side dish to rice and bread.

Wherever you travel in the Middle East I guarantee you'll find okra stewed in a tomato mixture with onions and spices – it's a favourite. Here, I've added potatoes to make a more substantial dish, but I still think of this as a sharing dish to serve alongside other vegetable dishes and rice and/or flatbreads. Or, serve it at room temperature, drizzled with olive oil and with thick Greek yogurt alongside. I've used a traditional vegetable combination here, but you have endless options. Replace the floury potatoes with sweet potatoes, or use diced aubergine and/or courgettes. Finely shredded mint for the garnish is a good option, too. For more variety you can also replace the Yemeni Curry Powder with *baharat* (page 276).

Stewed Okra & Potatoes
tabeekh

2 tablespoons olive oil
3 garlic cloves, chopped
1 long, thin green chilli, finely chopped
1 onion, chopped
1 tablespoon Yemeni Curry Powder (page 275)
1½ teaspoons ground turmeric
1 tomato, chopped
125ml passata
250ml water, or as needed
1 celery stalk, trimmed and chopped
250g okra pods, stem ends removed and the pods chopped
150g floury potatoes, such as King Edwards, peeled and cut into 1cm cubes
sea salt
chopped coriander or flat-leaf parsley, to garnish

Heat the oil in a saucepan over a medium-high heat. Add the garlic, chilli and onion with a pinch of salt and fry, stirring often, until the onion is softened. Add the curry powder and ground turmeric and stir for 30 seconds.

Add the tomato and continue stirring just until it starts to soften. Stir in the passata with a couple tablespoons of the water to make sure you get it all out of the measuring jug. Add the celery, okra and potatoes with a pinch of salt, stirring them into the tomato mixture.

Stir in the remaining water, adding more if needed so the vegetables are just submerged. Bring to the boil, then turn the heat to low and leave the vegetables to simmer, uncovered, for 15 minutes, adding a splash of water to cover the vegetables if necessary, until they are all tender – if the potatoes aren't submerged, they take much longer to cook. Taste and adjust the salt, if necessary. Garnish with coriander or parsley and serve.

Serves 4

Split yellow peas are a staple of domestic cooking in Yemen and throughout the Middle East. This is an everyday family recipe, especially popular during Ramadan, when it's used to break the fast. This soup can be served with bread or rice, but I serve it with toasted pitta breads.

Yemeni Lentil Soup
jizan shwrbat aleads

200g split yellow peas (*toor daal* or pigeon peas), rinsed and soaked in cold water to cover for 20 minutes
1½ tablespoons olive oil
3 dried bay leaves
3 garlic cloves, finely chopped
1 large onion, finely chopped
1 tablespoon Yemeni Curry Powder (page 275)
1 teaspoon smoked paprika
½ teaspoon ground cumin
1.3 litres water
freshly squeezed lemon juice, to taste
sea salt
chopped coriander or flat-leaf parsley, to garnish

To serve
pitta breads, toasted
hilbeh (page 248), optional
zhoug (page 249), optional

First, cook the split yellow peas. Drain, then put them in a large saucepan with a lid over a high heat with plenty of water to cover and a pinch of salt. Bring to the boil, skimming the surface as necessary, and cook for 20 minutes or until just tender. Drain well and set aside.

Meanwhile, heat the oil in a large saucepan over a medium-high heat. Add the bay leaves and stir for 30 seconds or so to flavour the oil. Add the garlic and onion with a good pinch of salt and fry, stirring often, until the onion is softened. Add the curry powder, smoked paprika and cumin, and stir for 30 seconds to cook the ground spices.

Add the water and the split yellow peas and bring to the boil. Reduce the heat, cover the pan and leave to simmer for 1¼ hours or until the split peas break down to form a thick soup. Add lemon juice to taste and adjust the salt, if necessary. Garnish with the coriander or parsley and serve with plenty of pitta bread and the *hibeh* and *zhoug* on the side, if you like.

This chunky soup is a meal in a bowl. I've made it with a combination of vegetables I particularly like, but feel free to add whatever you like. Any canned pulse can be substituted for the chickpeas.

Hawaij Vegetable Soup
hasa 'alkhidar har

2 tablespoons olive oil
1 onion, finely chopped
400g butternut squash, peeled, deseeded and finely diced
2 large carrots, peeled, halved lengthwise and cut into 0.5cm slices
2 floury potatoes, such as King Edwards, peeled and finely chopped
2 tablespoons Yemeni Curry Powder (page 275)
1 can (400g) chickpeas, drained and rinsed
3 celery stalks, trimmed and chopped
2 tomatoes, chopped
1.2 litres vegetable stock, ideally home-made (page 282), or water
sea salt

To serve
natural full-fat yogurt
smoked paprika
chopped mint, coriander or flat-leaf parsley leaves
olive oil, optional
flatbread, such a pittas

Heat the oil in a large saucepan with a lid over a medium-high heat. Add the onion with a pinch of salt and fry, stirring occasionally, until the onion is softened. Add the squash, carrots and potatoes, and stir for 1 minute so they are coated with the onions. Add the curry powder and stir for 30 seconds. The aroma should be wonderful at this point.

Stir in the chickpeas and celery, then add the tomatoes with a pinch of salt. Pour in the stock and bring to the boil. Reduce the heat, cover with the lid and leave the soup to simmer for 25–30 minutes until the vegetables are tender. Taste and adjust the salt, if necessary.

Ladle into bowls. Add a spoonful of yogurt to each, dust with paprika and sprinkle with the chopped mint, coriander or parsley. Drizzle with olive oil, if you like, and serve with plenty of flatbreads.

This particular recipe reminds of the India staple daal chawal, a combination of rice and lentils which the country lives off. The rice is cooked with all the spices like a pulao would be, but this is balanced by the beautiful flavours of the dried lime and baharat in the rice and the sweetness of the dried barberries and pomegranate molasses in the pulses. The floral notes added by the rosewater elevate this humble recipe to something very special. It's a celebration dish, and I love it.

Omani Rice with Mixed Pulses
quabuli

300g white basmati rice, rinsed under cold water until the water runs clear and soaked in cold water to cover for 30 minutes

3 tablespoons olive oil

1 garlic clove, chopped

1 onion, sliced

1 dried bay leaf

1 teaspoon cardamom seeds

¼ teaspoon black peppercorns

2–3 shards of cinnamon bark

1 dried lime, punctured all over with a sharp knife

1 tablespoon *baharat* (page 276)

1½ tablespoons sultanas

sea salt

For the pulses

200g split yellow peas (*toor daal* or pigeon peas), rinsed and soaked in cold water to cover for 20 minutes

100g split yellow mung dal (*moong daal*), rinsed and soaked in cold water to cover for 20 minutes

First, cook the pulses. Put the split yellow peas in one saucepan over a high heat with plenty of water to cover and a pinch of salt. Bring to the boil, skimming the surface, if necessary, and cook for 20 minutes or until just tender.

At the same time, put the split yellow mung dal and split red lentils in a separate pan over a high heat with plenty of water to cover and a pinch of salt. Bring to the boil, skimming the surface as necessary, and boil for 15 minutes or until both pulses are just tender. Strain each pan, reserving the liquid, and set all the pulses aside together.

Meanwhile, drain the rice and set aside.

Heat the 3 tablespoons oil in a flameproof casserole or large saucepan with a lid over a medium-high heat. Add the garlic and onion and fry, stirring, for 1 minute to cook out the raw flavour of the garlic. Add the bay leaf, cardamom seeds, peppercorns, cinnamon bark and dried lime, and continue stirring until the onions are light brown and the mixture is fragrant. At this point, I think the aromas smell almost like vanilla coming from the pan.

100g split red lentils (*masoor daal*), rinsed and soaked in cold water to cover for 20 minutes
1½ tablespoons olive oil
1 onion, thinly sliced
1 teaspoon *baharat* (page 276)
3 tablespoons dried barberries
1 tablespoon pomegranate molasses
½ teaspoon rosewater
2 tablespoons chopped coriander leaves, plus extra to garnish
pomegranate seeds, to garnish

Add the rice and *baharat* to the pan and stir them into the onion mixture for 1 minute. Add the sultanas and salt to taste. Pour in enough water to come 2.5cm above the surface of the rice and stir everything together. Bring to the boil and continue to boil, uncovered, just until the water goes below the surface. At that point turn the heat to the lowest possible setting, cover the surface of the rice with parchment paper and cover the pan with the lid. Use a heat diffuser under the pan if you have one. Leave the rice to simmer for a further 5–7 minutes, or until small holes appear on the surface, no water is left in the bottom of the pan and the texture is light and fluffy with separate grains. Do not uncover the pan and lift the paper to check the rice until after 5 minutes.

Meanwhile, prepare the mixed pulses. Heat the 1½ tablespoons oil in a large saucepan over a medium-high heat. Add the onion and fry, stirring often, until it is translucent. Add the cooked pulses, *baharat* and barberries with salt to taste, and stir together. Stir in 150ml of the reserved cooking liquid, the pomegranate molasses, rosewater and chopped coriander. Leave the pulses to bubble and thicken while the rice finishes cooking.

When you are ready to serve, fluff up the rice using 2 forks, put a portion of rice in each bowl and make a well in the centre. Spoon the lentils into the well and on top of the rice, then garnish with coriander leaves and pomegranate seeds.

Makes 8

I think these delicious breads are best served straight from the pan, but if you have the patience and want to cook them all first, just keep them warm by wrapping them in a clean tea towel or foil as you cook each one.

Omani Flatbreads
maldouf

75g pitted dates, chopped
250ml boiling water
280g chapati flour (*atta*) or plain wholemeal flour, plus extra for dusting
4 tablespoons ghee, at room temperature so it's liquid, plus extra for finishing
sea salt

Put the dates and boiling water in a blender or small food processor and process until smooth.

Put the flour and a pinch of salt in a large bowl and make a well in the centre. Add the ghee, followed by the date paste and stir together, drawing in the flour from the side of the bowl, until a soft dough forms. Knead the dough in the bowl. If it is too sticky, sprinkle with a little flour and continue kneading. Shape into a ball, cover the bowl and leave to rest for 10 minutes to activate the gluten in the flour.

When you are ready to make the breads, put the dough on a floured surface and pat into a log with an equal thickness. Cut into 8 equal pieces, then form each piece into a smooth ball. Put a generous amount of chapati flour in a small bowl.

Working with one dough ball at a time, place it in the extra chapati flour and press down. Flip it over and repeat on the other side. It should be fairly well coated at this point. Roll out into a 20cm circle, then gently slap the dough back and forth between your hands to remove the excess flour.

Meanwhile, heat a dry *tawa* (cast-iron flat pan) or non-stick frying pan over a medium-high heat. When the pan is hot, add a dough circle and leave to cook until it loses its raw appearance, has brown spots on the bottom and puffs up. Flip over and repeat. When the bread is speckled on both sides, brush the top with ghee. Flip it over, repeat on the other side and serve or keep warm while you cook the rest.

This style of cooking is very close to my heart. I absolutely adore cooking pulses and vegetables together, as you can see from the recipes in this book. The split yellow peas are an essential ingredient in this dish, but you can use any other vegetables that hold their shape during cooking instead of the aubergine. Pumpkin or courgette would also be good. You can also replace the tofu with another vegetarian protein, such as paneer, tempeh or seitan. Serve with a Middle Eastern flatbread, such as Omani Flatbread (page 258) or pitta bread.

Aubergine & Split Pea Stew
hisaan man biadhinjan walbazala

sunflower oil
1½ onions, finely chopped
250g aubergines, trimmed and cut into bite-sized pieces
250g firm tofu, patted dry and cut into bite-sized chunks
200g split yellow peas (*toor daal* or pigeon peas), rinsed and soaked in cold water to cover for 20 minutes
1 thick dried red chilli, left whole
1 tablespoon plus 1 teaspoon *baharat* (page 276)
1 teaspoon smoked paprika
¼ teaspoon ground nutmeg
about 250ml water
1 tablespoon sour pomegranate molasses – make sure you don't buy the sweet variety
sea salt

To garnish
thin aubergine slices, fried until tender
grated firm tofu

Heat 2 tablespoons oil in a large, deep frying pan with a lid over a medium-high heat. Add the onions with a pinch of salt and fry, stirring often, until they turn light brown. Keep an eye on the onions while you fry the aubergine and tofu because they can burn quickly.

Meanwhile, line a large plate with kitchen paper and set aside. Heat a thin layer of oil in another large frying pan over a medium-high heat. Add the aubergine pieces and fry, turning occasionally, until they are evenly browned. You're not cooking the aubergine completely at this point – they will finish looking later in the recipe – but you want to colour all the pieces. Cook in batches, adding more oil to the pan as necessary because aubergines really soaks it up. Remove the aubergine pieces from the pan and transfer to the plate to drain.

Heat another thin layer of oil in the pan, lower the heat, add the tofu pieces and fry, turning the pieces over until they are coloured all over. Remove from the pan, add to the aubergine and set aside.

When the onions have browned, add the split yellow peas and their soaking liquid. Bring to the boil and stir together until most of the liquid evaporates. Stir

chopped flat-leaf parsley
  or coriander leaves
full-fat natural yogurt, to serve,
  optional

in the red chilli, *baharat*, paprika and nutmeg, and continue stirring for 30 seconds to cook the ground spices. It should smell wonderful at this point.

Pour in enough water to cover the split peas and add salt to taste. Bring to the boil, then reduce the heat a little, cover the pan and leave to cook for about 15 minutes until the split peas are tender and the liquid is absorbed. Remove the chilli and discard.

Stir in half the fresh water, scraping the bottom of the pan – you don't want to lose any of the flavour from the caramelisation. Add the aubergines and tofu and the remaining water if the stew is too thick. Return to the boil, stirring, then lower the heat and leave to simmer until the aubergines are tender.

Stir in the pomegranate molasses. Garnish and serve, with yogurt on the side, if you like.

Left: Aubergine & Split
Pea Stew (page 260)
Right: White Bean Curry
(page 264)

Serves 4

You might be surprised to see a Middle Eastern dish with Indian curry powder, but India actually has strong cultural and political links with Iraq, so there has been quite a bit of culinary cross-fertilisation.

White Bean Curry
hisaan man fasulya abyad

250g dried butter beans, rinsed and soaked overnight in cold water to cover
sunflower oil
1½ onions, chopped
200g floury potatoes, such as King Edwards, peeled and cut into bite-sized pieces
1 garlic clove, chopped
2 teaspoons Madras curry powder, mild or hot, as you like
½ can (400g) peeled chopped tomatoes
5 tablespoons passata
125ml water
sea salt and freshly ground black pepper
chopped coriander or flat-leaf parsley leaves, to garnish

First, cook the butter beans. Drain the beans and rinse. Place them in a lidded saucepan with cold water to cover, then cover the pan and bring to the boil. Uncover the pan and boil hard for 10 minutes, then skim the surface. Reduce the heat and leave to simmer, partially covered, for about 40 minutes until almost tender – they will be cooking further later in the recipe so don't cook them completely at this point. Strain and set aside, reserving the cooking liquid.

Heat 1 tablespoon oil in a large saucepan over a medium-high heat. Add two-thirds of the chopped onions and fry, stirring often, until they are translucent. Add the potatoes with a pinch of salt to taste and stir around until they are coated with the onions. Pour in enough of the bean cooking liquid to cover the potatoes. Bring to the boil and boil for 8–10 minutes until the potatoes are beginning to soften. They are cooked for a further 10 minutes later in the recipe so you don't want them completely tender now.

Meanwhile, heat 1 tablespoon oil in a large frying pan over a medium-high heat. Add the remaining onions and fry, stirring often, until they start to soften. Add the garlic and continue frying until the onions are translucent. Add the curry powder and continue stirring for 30 seconds to cook the spices. Watch closely because the garlic and spices can burn quickly. Stir in the beans with salt to taste, remembering that the liquid the potatoes are cooking in has already been salted. Add the tomatoes and passata.

Tip this mixture into the pan with the potatoes and stir together. Add the 125ml fresh water and return to the boil. Reduce the heat and leave to simmer for 10 minutes, stirring occasionally, or until the potatoes and beans are tender.

If the stew is too thick you can stir in some extra water. Just before serving, add black pepper to taste and adjust the salt, if necessary. Sprinkle with coriander or parsley and serve.

This is my idea of a perfect everyday family meal, as it can be enjoyed hot or at room temperature, and certainly isn't harmed by making in advance for reheating. It pairs well with Stir-fried Kale with Coconut (page 200) and pitta bread or any other flatbread.

Lebanese Baked Vegetable Stew
maghmour

2½ tablespoons olive oil
1 onion, thinly sliced
2 garlic cloves, finely chopped
250ml passata
1 can (400g) peeled chopped
　tomatoes
4 tablespoons chopped
　coriander leaves
1 teaspoon *baharat* (page 276)
½ teaspoon ground cumin
½ teaspoon smoked paprika
⅛ teaspoon ground cinnamon
150g frozen sweetcorn kernels
1 can (400g) chickpeas, drained
　and rinsed
15cm piece of trimmed leek,
　sliced and rinsed
10 okra pods, stem ends
　removed and the pods
　chopped
2 baby aubergines, or ½ large
　aubergine, cut into bite-sized
　pieces
1 celery stalk, sliced
1 green pepper, cored,
　deseeded and chopped
250ml water
1 tomato, chopped
75g Cheddar cheese
sea salt

Preheat the oven to 200°C/Fan 180°C/Gas 6.

Heat the oil in a large saucepan over a medium-high heat. Add the onion and fry, stirring often, until the onion starts to colour. Add the garlic and continue stirring until the onion is lightly browned.

Stir in the passata, canned tomatoes and 2 tablespoons of the coriander leaves, and bring to the boil, using your spoon to lightly crush the tomato pieces. Stir in the *baharat*, ground cumin, paprika, cinnamon and a pinch of salt, then add the sweetcorn and chickpeas and stir for 30 seconds to cook the spices. Reduce the heat and add the leek, okra, aubergines, celery and green pepper, and stir together. Stir in the water, chopped tomato, remaining 2 tablespoons coriander leaves and salt to taste, and return to the boil.

Pour into an ovenproof serving dish, cover the dish with foil, then place on a baking tray. Transfer to the oven and cook for 25 minutes. Remove from the oven and scatter over the cheese. Return to the oven and cook for another 20 minutes or until all the vegetables are tender.

fo

sides &
undations

Toasting & Grinding Seeds, Spices & Dried Herbs

Whole seeds and spices are often toasted and ground before use to intensify their flavours. I do this with most of the spice powders in this book, and specifically with cumin and fennel seeds.

Put the seeds and spices in a dry frying pan over a medium heat and toast by stirring until whole spices become aromatic and seeds start to pop. Watch closely so they do not burn. Immediately tip them out of the pan and leave to cool before grinding. Spices generally contain a great deal of oil, so by leaving them to cool before grinding, the powder won't stick to the bottom of the grinder.

Dried herbs, such as bay leaves, are also toasted to remove any moisture they might retain before they are ground.

Grinding spices is an essential technique in many of the cuisines in this book, and seeds and spices can be ground with or without having been toasted first. To grind seeds, other spices and dried herbs, use a spice grinder or coffee grinder, or use a pestle and mortar. Depending on the quantity, you can also use a small food processor. If using a pestle and mortar you'll probably have to pass the powder through a fine sieve. This is especially true when the mixture contains cassia or cinnamon bark regardless of what you use to grind it.

Ground Toasted Cumin Seeds
Many of my recipes use ground cumin, which you can buy. For other recipes, however, I specify ground toasted cumin seeds, which you have to prepare yourself. Toast the cumin seeds as explained above, then grind them to a powder. This is best done just before using, so I recommend a pestle and mortar, as the quantity is usually too small to work well in a spice or coffee grinder.

Ground Fennel Seeds
The flavour of freshly ground fennel seeds is far superior to any ground fennel you buy. Use a pestle and mortar and grind them just before using.

Atul's Garam Masala

Makes about 40g

5 green cardamom pods, bruised
5 cloves
1 dried bay leaf
1 black cardamom pod, bruised
½ dried red chilli
1cm piece of cinnamon bark
4 tablespoons coriander seeds
1 tablespoon cumin seeds
¼ teaspoon black peppercorns
¾ teaspoon dried edible
  rose petals
¼ teaspoon ground ginger
⅛ nutmeg

Heat a dry frying pan over a medium heat. Add the green cardamom pods, cloves, bay leaf, black cardamom pod, dried red chilli, cinnamon bark, coriander seeds, cumin seeds and black peppercorns, and stir until aromatic and the seeds start to pop. Watch closely so they do not burn. Immediately tip them on to a plate.

When all the spices and bay leaf are cool, transfer them to a spice grinder or coffee grinder, or use a pestle and mortar. Add the dried rose petals and ground ginger and grate in the nutmeg, then grind to a fine powder. Pass through a fine sieve. Store in an airtight container in a dark place and use within 6 months.

Nepalese Garam Masala

Makes about 20g

4cm piece of cinnamon bark
1 tablespoon green cardamom
  pods, bruised
1 tablespoon coriander seeds
1 tablespoon cumin seeds
½ teaspoon cloves
½ teaspoon timur (*timut*)
  peppercorns, or use Szechuan
  peppercorns
1 dried bay leaf
½ teaspoon ground ginger
½ teaspoon grated nutmeg

Heat a dry frying pan over a medium heat. Add the cinnamon bark, green cardamom pods, coriander seeds, cumin seeds, cloves and timur peppercorns, and stir until they have a smoky aroma and the seeds start to pop. Watch closely that they do not burn. Immediately tip them on to a plate.

When the spices and bay leaf are cool, transfer them to a spice grinder or coffee grinder, or use a pestle and mortar. Add the bay leaf, ground ginger and grated nutmeg, and grind to a fine powder. Pass the powder through a fine sieve. Store in an airtight container in a dark place and use within 6 months.

Sindhi Garam Masala

Use this recipe for an authentic Sindhi flavour. In a pinch you can use Atul's Garam Masala (page 271) or an ordinary garam masala in any recipe that calls for this specific mix.

Makes about 25g

2½ teaspoons green cardamom pods, bruised
4 black cardamom pods, bruised
1 dried bay leaf
½ star anise
4cm piece of cassia or cinnamon bark
1½ teaspoons cloves
1½ teaspoons black peppercorns
¾ teaspoon aniseeds or fennel seeds
¾ teaspoon caraway seeds
¾ teaspoons cumin seeds
1½ teaspoons edible rose petals
⅛ nutmeg

Heat a dry frying pan over a medium heat. Add the green and black cardamom pods, bay leaf, star anise and cassia bark, and stir until aromatic. Immediately tip them on to a plate. Add the cloves, peppercorns, aniseeds, caraway seeds and cumin seeds to pan, and stir until aromatic and the seeds are beginning to pop. Watch closely so they don't burn. Immediately tip on to the plate.

When the spices and bay leaf are cool, transfer them into a spice grinder or coffee grinder, or use a pestle and mortar. Add the rose petals and grate in the nutmeg, then grind to a fine powder. Pass the powder through a fine sieve. Store in an airtight container in a dark place and use within 6 months.

Sri Lankan Toasted Curry Powder

Makes about 55g

50g coriander seeds
5 green cardamom pods, bruised
3 cloves
2.5cm piece of cinnamon bark
1 teaspoon cumin seeds
1 teaspoon fennel seeds
½ teaspoon fenugreek seeds

Heat a dry frying pan over a medium heat. Add the coriander seeds, cardamom pods, cloves, cinnamon bark, cumin seeds, fennel seeds and fenugreek seeds, and stir until aromatic and the seeds start to pop. Immediately tip them on to a plate.

When the spices are cool, transfer them to a spice grinder or coffee grinder, or use a pestle and mortar, and grind until a fine powder forms. Pass the powder through a fine sieve. Store in an airtight container in a dark place and use within 6 months.

East African Curry Powder

Curry powders from East African countries, including Ethiopia, Kenya, Malawi and Uganda, will each be slightly different. To keep things simple, I've created a powder I think represents the essence of the region's curries, rather than using a separate powder for each.

Makes about 60g

2 tablespoons red chilli powder
1 tablespoon cardamom seeds
1 tablespoon ground cinnamon
1 tablespoon ground turmeric
1 teaspoon ground ginger

Mix all the ingredients together, then store in an airtight container in a dark place and use within 6 months.

South African Curry Powder

Makes about 50g

40g cumin seeds
25g fennel seeds
10g dried peri-peri chillies
2cm piece of cinnamon bark
1 clove
2 teaspoons black peppercorns
¾ teaspoon ground turmeric

Heat a dry frying pan over a medium heat. Add the cumin and fennel seeds and dry-fry, stirring, until they are aromatic and start to pop. Immediately tip them on to a plate. One by one add the remaining spices, except the ground turmeric, to the pan and toast, stirring, until aromatic. Add to the plate. Watch closely so none of the spices burn.

When the spices are cool, transfer them to a spice grinder or coffee grinder, or use a pestle and mortar. Add the ground turmeric and grind to a fine powder. Pass through a fine sieve. Store in an airtight container in a dark place and use within 6 months.

Malaysian
Kurma Powder

Makes about 40g

10cm piece of cinnamon bark
10 green cardamom pods,
   bruised
4 cloves
2 star anise
1 teaspoon black peppercorns
4 tablespoons coriander seeds
2 teaspoon aniseeds
2 teaspoon cumin seeds
½ nutmeg
2 teaspoons ground turmeric

Heat a dry, large wok over a medium heat. Add the cinnamon bark, green cardamom pods, cloves, star anise and peppercorns, and stir until aromatic. Immediately tip them on to a plate. Add the coriander seeds, aniseeds and cumin seeds to the wok and stir until they pop and darken. Add them to the plate. Watch closely so nothing burns.

When all the spices are cool, transfer them to a spice grinder or coffee grinder, or use a pestle and mortar. Grate in the nutmeg and add the ground turmeric, then grind to a fine powder. Pass the powder through a fine sieve and store in an airtight container in a dark place and use within 6 months.

Malay Curry
Powder

Makes about 30g

2.5cm piece of cinnamon bark
5 cloves
5 black peppercorns
2 green cardamom pods, bruised
3 dried red chillies
1 star anise
2 tablespoons coriander seeds
2 tablespoons cumin seeds
½ teaspoon fennel seeds
½ teaspoon ground turmeric

Heat a dry wok over a medium heat. Add all the whole spices and the seeds and stir until aromatic and the seeds start to pop. Watch closely so nothing burns. Immediately tip them on to the plate.

When the spices are cool, transfer them into a spice grinder or coffee grinder, or use a pestle and mortar. Add the ground turmeric and grind to a fine powder. Pass the powder through a fine sieve. Store in an airtight container in a dark place and use within 6 months.

Yemeni Curry Powder

When I'm toasting this combination of spices it immediately transports me to Arab spice markets. This is evocative of the heady aroma you always experience throughout the Middle East, regardless of which country you are in.

Makes 40g

2 tablespoons cumin seeds
1 tablespoon coriander seeds
1 tablespoon black peppercorns
1 teaspoon green cardamom
  pods, bruised
1 teaspoon cloves
1 tablespoon ground turmeric

Heat a dry frying pan over a medium heat. Add the cumin and coriander seeds, peppercorns, cardamom pods and cloves, and stir until the spices are aromatic and darker and the seeds pop. Immediately tip them on to a plate. When the spices are cool, transfer them to a spice grinder or coffee grinder, or use a pestle and mortar. Add the ground turmeric and grind to a fine powder. Pass through a fine sieve if you used a pestle and mortar. Store in an airtight container in a dark place to use within 6 months.

Parsi Masala

I get nostalgic with the smell of this spice mix – some wonderful foodie memories are associated with this combination of spices.

Makes about 70g

5 dried red chillies
3 cloves
2 dried Indian bay leaves
1 black cardamom pod, bruised
1 star anise
50g coriander seeds
2 teaspoons green cardamom
  pods, bruised
1½ teaspoons cumin seeds
1 teaspoon black peppercorns
½ teaspoon fenugreek seeds
½ teaspoon black mustard seeds
1½ teaspoons ground turmeric
¾ teaspoon ground ginger

Heat a dry frying pan over a medium heat. Add the dried red chillies, cloves, bay leaves, black cardamom pod, star anise, coriander seeds, green cardamom pods, cumin seeds, peppercorns, fenugreek seeds and mustard seeds, and stir until aromatic and the seeds start popping. Watch closely to make sure they do not burn. Immediately tip them on to a plate.

When the bay leaves and spices are cool, transfer them to a coffee grinder or spice grinder, or use a pestle and mortar. Add the ground turmeric and ground ginger and grind to a fine powder. You might have to do this in batches. Pass the powder through a fine sieve. Store in an airtight container in a dark place and use within 6 months.

Baharat

Baharat is widely available but I wanted to make my own version when I was developing these recipes. Unlike most of the spice powders I make regularly, the spices in this mix are ground without being toasted first. I had to resist the temptation to follow my instinct, but I wanted to respect the Middle Eastern tradition.

Makes about 40g

10 cloves
8 green cardamom pods
2 tablespoons coriander seeds
1 tablespoon allspice berries
1 tablespoon cumin seeds
1 tablespoon black peppercorns
1 heaped teaspoon ground
  cinnamon

Put the cloves, green cardamom pods, coriander seeds, allspice berries, cumin seeds and black peppercorns in a spice grinder or coffee grinder, or use a pestle and mortar, and grind to a fine powder. Add the ground cinnamon and grind again. If using a pestle and mortar, pass through a fine sieve. Store in an airtight container in a dark place and use within 6 months.

Berbere Spice Powder

This has a fiery flavour that adds a real zing to any Middle Eastern and barbecue recipes.

Makes about 45g

12 green cardamom pods,
  bruised
6 dried red bird's-eye chillies
2 teaspoons coriander seeds
2 teaspoons cumin seeds
2 teaspoons fenugreek seeds
1 teaspoon black peppercorns
½ teaspoon cloves
2 teaspoons smoked paprika
2 teaspoons sweet paprika
1 teaspoon ground cinnamon
1 teaspoon ground ginger
1 teaspoon ground nutmeg
1 teaspoon sea salt

Heat a dry frying pan over a medium heat. Add the green cardamom pods, bird's-eye chillies, coriander seeds, cumin seeds, fenugreek seeds, peppercorns and cloves, and stir until aromatic and the seeds start to pop. Watch closely so none of the spices burn. Immediately tip them on to a plate.

When the spices are cool, transfer them to a spice grinder or coffee grinder, or use a pestle and mortar. Add the smoked paprika, sweet paprika, ground cinnamon, ground ginger, ground nutmeg and salt, and grind to a fine powder. If using a pestle and mortar, pass through a fine sieve. Store in an airtight container in a dark place and use within 6 months.

Cambodian Spice Paste

This is a traditional spice paste that adds an authentic flavour to Cambodian recipes. Although this recipe makes more than is used in the Khmer Vegetable Curry (page 38), the leftovers can be frozen – I recommend freezing the paste in the individual compartments of an ice-cube tray and then transferring to a freezer-proof bag. The compartments on my ice-cube tray each hold 2 tablespoons so I can quickly grab the amount I need.

Makes about 100g

1 dried long, thin red chilli, soaked in hot water to cover for 20 minutes
2cm piece of galangal, peeled and roughly chopped
15g fresh turmeric, peeled and roughly chopped, or ½ teaspoon ground turmeric
5 black peppercorns
3 fresh or freeze-dried Makrut lime leaves, fine central ribs removed
2 green cardamom pods
2 garlic cloves, chopped
1½ large lemongrass stalks, outer layers removed and the stalks bashed and chopped
1 small shallot, chopped
1 tablespoon sunflower oil
½ small bunch of coriander with roots and stems, chopped and rinsed
1 teaspoon vegetarian fish sauce
⅛ teaspoon coriander seeds
⅛ teaspoon fennel seeds

When the chilli is rehydrated, strain it, reserving the soaking liquid. Remove the stem end and deseed the chilli, then transfer it to a food processor.

Add all the remaining ingredients to the food processor and process until a paste forms, scraping down the side of the bowl as necessary, and adding a few tablespoons of the soaking water to make a smoother paste. Alternatively, pound the ingredients together with a pestle and mortar. This will keep in a covered container in the fridge for up to 1 week, or can be frozen for up to 3 months.

Thai Green Curry Paste

Makes about 250g

1 teaspoon coriander seeds
1 teaspoon cumin seeds
20 white peppercorns
100g green Thai chillies,
  deseeded and chopped
3cm piece of galangal, peeled
  and coarsely chopped, or use
  extra ginger
2cm piece of fresh ginger,
  peeled and coarsely chopped
200g red shallots, chopped
12 garlic cloves, coarsely
  chopped
½ lemongrass stalk, outer layers
  removed and the stalk bashed
  and chopped
8 fresh Makrut lime leaves, fine
  central ribs removed and
  chopped
2 tablespoons chopped
  coriander roots, or use
  coriander stalks
2 teaspoons vegetarian fish
  sauce
2 teaspoons peeled and
  chopped fresh turmeric, or
  ½ teaspoon ground turmeric
a large handful of Thai or
  ordinary basil leaves
2–3 tablespoons water, as
  needed

Heat a dry frying pan over a medium heat. Add the coriander seeds, cumin seeds and peppercorns, and stir until aromatic and the seeds start to pop. Immediately tip the spices on to a plate.

When the spices are cool, transfer them to a spice grinder or coffee grinder, or use a pestle and mortar. Grind to a fine powder. Pass the powder through a fine sieve if you used a pestle and mortar.

Transfer the ground spices and remaining ingredients, except the water, to a food processor, then process until a coarse paste forms, scraping down the side of the bowl as necessary, and gradually adding the water to break down the ingredients to make a smoother paste. Store in a covered container in the fridge for up to 1 week or freeze for up to 3 months.

Thai Red
Curry Paste

Makes about 250g

5 cloves
1 tablespoon coriander seeds
1 teaspoon cumin seeds
1 teaspoon white peppercorns
100g fresh Thai red chillies,
   deseeded and chopped
½ nutmeg, grated
4 shallots, finely chopped
3 garlic cloves, chopped
2 lemongrass stalks, outer layers
   removed and the stalks bashed
   and coarsely chopped
freshly grated zest of 2 unwaxed
   Makrut limes or ordinary limes
½ teaspoon vegetarian fish
   sauce
¼ teaspoon sea salt
2–3 tablespoons water, as
   needed

Heat a dry frying pan over a medium heat. Add the cloves, coriander seeds, cumin seeds and peppercorns, and stir until aromatic and the seeds start to pop. Immediately tip them on to a plate.

When the spices are cool, transfer then to a spice grinder or coffee grinder, or use a pestle and mortar, and grind to a fine powder. Pass the powder through a fine sieve if you used a pestle and mortar.

Transfer the ground spices and remaining ingredients, except the water, to a food processor, then process until a coarse paste forms, scraping down the side of the bowl as necessary, and gradually adding the water to break down the ingredients to form a smoother paste. Store in a covered container in the fridge for up to 1 week, or freeze for up to 3 months.

Onion Paste

Makes about 550g

1kg onions, peeled and halved
60ml sunflower oil
200g Ginger-Garlic Paste
  (page 281)
2 teaspoons sea salt

Put the onions in a large heavy-based saucepan with a lid with water to cover. Cover the pan and bring to the boil, then simmer for 8–10 minutes until the onions are soft enough to easily slide a knife into them. Cooking them first removes the bitterness. Drain well and leave to cool. When cool enough to handle, roughly chop and pat dry.

Heat the oil in a large frying pan, ideally non-stick, over a medium-high heat. Add the onions, ginger-garlic paste and salt, and fry, stirring frequently, for 25 minutes, or until the onions are very light brown. Don't be alarmed if they appear to have a slight green tinge while they are cooking. Watch very closely towards the end of the cooking time so the mixture doesn't catch and burn, which can happen quickly. If necessary, stir in a little water, scraping the bottom of the pan. Be warned, if the onions do burn, you'll have to throw them out and start over – there isn't any way to rescue them.

Transfer the mixture to a food processor while it's still warm and process to a fine paste. Leave to cool completely, then store in a covered container in the fridge for up to 1 week, or freeze for up to 3 months.

Ginger-Garlic Paste

Makes about 225g

2 large garlic heads, 75g each,
 separated into cloves and
 peeled
150g fresh ginger, peeled weight,
 roughly chopped
2 tablespoons water

Put the garlic cloves, ginger and water in a food processor fitted with a chopping blade, and process, scraping down the side of the bowl as necessary, until a paste forms. This keeps in a covered container in the fridge for up to 1 week, or it can be frozen for up to 3 months.

Ginger Paste

Makes about 300g

300g fresh ginger, peeled and
 roughly chopped
2 tablespoons water

Put the ginger and water in a food processor or blender and process, scraping down the side of the bowl as necessary, until a paste forms. This keeps in a covered container in the fridge for up to 1 week, or it can be frozen for up to 3 months.

Vegetable Stock

A mantra of every well-run professional kitchen is that nothing goes to waste, a principle I try to encourage everyone in my house to follow at well. Even your vegetable trimmings can be put to good use in a pot of flavoursome vegetable stock – it's what we do at the restaurants (see Atul's tip, below). A good, home-made stock is the backbone of so many recipes in this book. Of course, you can use a stock cube or the pots of concentrated stock, but I recommend you make up a big batch of this basic stock and freeze in smaller portions.

Makes about 2 litres

2 tablespoons sunflower oil
4 celery sticks, with leaves, chopped
2 carrots, scrubbed and roughly chopped
2 onions, finely chopped
1 leek, sliced and rinsed
2.2 litres water
12 black peppercorns, lightly crushed
6 garlic cloves, crushed
1 bay leaf and several sprigs of parsley and thyme tied together
1 tomato, chopped, optional
sea salt

Heat the oil in a large saucepan with a lid over a medium-high heat. Stir in the celery, carrots, onions and leek with a pinch of salt, then reduce the heat to low, cover the pan and leave the vegetables to sweat for 10–15 minutes until very soft.

Pour the water into the pan, add the remaining ingredients, including the tomato, if using and ½ teaspoon salt. Turn up the heat and bring to the boil, skimming the surface as necessary. Reduce the heat to low, partially cover the pan and when the liquid is clear leave it to simmer for 20 minutes.

Drain the stock into a bowl and discard all the flavouring vegetables. The stock is now ready to use, or it can be left to cool completely and stored in a covered container in the fridge for up to 2 days, or frozen for up to 6 months.

● atul's tip

Almost any vegetable can be used in stock, but avoid potatoes, as they make it cloudy. Onion skins give the clear broth a pleasing golden hue if you are using in a recipe, such as Vegetable Noodle Soup (page 188). Take care not to over-salt the stock – most likely it will be used in a recipe with salt and other seasonings.

Basmati Rice

Cooking basmati rice that is light and fluffy with separate grains is really a two-stage process – the preparation and the actual cooking. The preparation begins with rinsing the rice to remove the excess starch, then soaking the rice in water to cover, which enables the water to be absorbed into the centre of each grain so they cook evenly. I notice many supermarket brands omit this step on the package instructions.

For brown basmati rice, follow the recipe below, but boil for 14–16 minutes until tender.

Serves 4

200g white basmati rice
sea salt

Tip the rice into a sieve and rinse under the cold tap until the water runs clear. Transfer to a bowl with water to cover and leave to soak for 30 minutes. When you are ready to cook, bring a saucepan of salted water to the boil. Drain the rice, then add it to the boiling water and boil for 6–8 minutes until tender. Drain well.

Jasmine Rice

I love jasmine rice in any form. Brown jasmine rice has a slight nutty flavour that I like very much. Cook as below, but simmer for 14–16 minutes.

Serves 4

200g Thai jasmine rice
sea salt

Tip the rice into a sieve and rinse under the cold tap until the water runs clear. Bring a saucepan of salted water to the boil. Add the rice, turn the heat to medium and simmer for 10–12 minutes until it is tender. Drain well and return to the pan. Place a clean tea towel over the rice, cover the pan and leave the rice to stand for 3 minutes. Fluff the grains with fork and it's ready to serve.

Sticky Rice

Oriental sticky rice, like basmati rice, is soaked before cooking to enable the water to be absorbed to the centre of each grain to make them tender and evenly cooked. Japanese chefs always use a small wooden paddle to serve sticky rice so the edge of a metal spoon doesn't damage the grains.

Serves 4

320g short-grain sticky rice
440ml water

Tip the rice into a sieve and rinse under the cold tap until the water runs clear. Transfer to a bowl, cover with fresh cold water and leave to soak for 30 minutes, then drain well.

Transfer the rice to a saucepan with a lid and add the water. Cover the pan and bring to the boil, then turn the heat to low and simmer for 10 minutes. Turn off the heat and leave the rice to stand for a further 10 minutes, with the pan still covered. It should now be tender and ready to serve.

Oat & Semolina Pancakes

jaee aur suji ke chille

Makes 6

200g oats, ground to a powder
   in a spice grinder or food
   processor
150g full-fat natural yogurt
100g fine semolina
2 garlic cloves, very finely
   chopped, or 1 teaspoon garlic
   powder
1cm piece of fresh ginger,
   peeled and finely chopped
2 teaspoons cumin seeds
1–2 long, thin green chillies,
   finely chopped, to taste
2 tablespoons chopped
   coriander leaves
500ml water
sea salt
vegetable oil
Tomato Salsa (page 292) or your
   favourite chutney, to serve

Put all the ingredients, except the vegetable oil and tomato salsa, with salt to taste in a bowl and whisk to make a smooth batter. Leave the batter to rest, uncovered, at room temperature for 4 hours. If not using immediately, cover the bowl and leave the batter the fridge for up to 24 hours until required.

When you are ready to cook the pancakes, heat a non-stick frying pan over a medium-high heat. Add 1 teaspoon of oil and brush all over the base of the pan. Add a 150ml ladleful of batter and spread it out to about 20cm in diameter, using the bottom of the ladle. Cook for 2 minutes, or until bubbles start appearing on the surface and the pancake is crisping and browning on the underside. Flip it over and cook on the other side for 1 minute.

Use a spatula to loosen it from the edge and slide the pancake on to a plate. These lose their heat quickly and become solid, so they are best served immediately, one by one, while you continue to cook the remaining batter. Alternatively, cover with a clean tea towel and keep warm until all are cooked. Serve with the tomato salsa – or any chutney of your choice.

Hoppers

These fermented, leavened bowl-like rice pancakes are a staple of Sri Lankan meals, served as an accompaniment to curries, rolled or folded, dipped into a curry and eaten with your hands, or for breakfast (see the variation, below), with a soft-cooked egg in the middle. Hoppers should have a soft, spongy texture with a crisp edge.

Makes about 8

200g rice flour
1 teaspoon grated jaggery
   or Demerara sugar
1 teaspoon fast-action
   dried yeast
500ml coconut milk
50ml warm water
rapeseed oil, for frying
sea salt

Put the rice flour, jaggery, yeast and a pinch of salt in a large bowl and stir together. Make a well in the centre. Gradually whisk in the coconut milk and then the water until combined and smooth. Cover with a tea towel and leave at room temperature to ferment for 2 hours, or leave in the fridge overnight or up to 3 days. Remove the batter from the fridge about 1 hour before cooking so it returns to room temperature.

When ready to cook, whisk the batter again until smooth. Heat a hopper pan or a small wok that can be covered over a medium-high heat. When it is very hot, using folded kitchen paper, wipe the pan generously with oil.

Using a 100ml ladle, pour a ladleful of the batter into the pan and swirl around to make a bowl-shaped pancake that comes up the side of the pan. Return the pan to the heat. Cook, uncovered, for 1 minute. Cover and cook for a further 2–3 minutes, or until the hopper base is cooked and the edges begin to turn golden brown and become lacy. Loosen the edge, remove the hopper from the pan and serve immediately. Repeat to use all the remaining batter.

● variation: egg hoppers

If you want to enjoy these for breakfast – as Sri Lankans do – after you add the batter to the pan and swirl it around, crack an egg into the centre, taking care not to break the yolk. Cover the pan and cook over a low heat until the egg is cooked to your liking.

Naans

It's virtually impossible in a domestic kitchen to replicate the slightly charred texture you get on naans cooked in a tandoor oven at Indian restaurants, although I find that a pizza stone works quite well. If you want more colour to the breads, after they're baked, put them under a preheated grill for a minute or two – just don't take your eyes off them, because they can burn quickly.

Makes 8

450g strong white flour, plus extra for kneading and rolling out
2 teaspoons fine sea salt or table salt
2 teaspoons sugar
1 tablespoon instant dried yeast
150ml milk, warm
2 tablespoons full-fat natural yogurt
45g ghee or butter, melted
2 tablespoons poppy seeds, optional
1 tablespoon sesame seeds, optional

Sift the flour, salt and sugar into a mixing bowl, and stir in the yeast. Make a well in the centre. Add the warm milk, yogurt and 2 tablespoons of the melted ghee, then mix together to make a soft dough. Turn out on to a lightly floured surface and knead for 8–10 minutes until smooth and elastic. Roll into a ball.

Lightly dust the bowl with flour. Return the dough to the bowl, cover with a damp tea towel and leave in a warm place for 1–2 hours, or until it is doubled in size.

Divide the dough into 8 equal pieces and shape each into a ball, then cover with a damp tea towel and leave to rest in a warm place for 10 minutes. Using a lightly floured rolling pin, roll out each ball into a circle on a lightly floured surface, then pull out one side to make a teardrop shape.

Meanwhile, preheat the oven to 220°C/Fan 200°C/Gas 7.

Mix together the poppy and sesame seeds, if using. Brush the remaining melted ghee on the naans and sprinkle with the seeds. Place on baking sheets and bake for 5–7 minutes until brown specks appear on the surface. If the breads aren't brown enough, put them under a preheated grill for a minute or so. Serve hot.

Chapatis

Bread is sometimes referred to as the 'third hand' in India, especially in the north, where it is a staple. Used as a utensil to scoop up gravy or dal, it also contrasts with, and enhances the food. *Roti* and chapati are two names for the same bread made with Indian *atta* flour, a type of wholewheat flour made from a wheat that is low in gluten and soft textured. Indian cooks are adept at lifting the chapati from the hot surface to check the brown spots underneath. Unless you have asbestos fingers, I suggest you use tongs to turn the breads.

Makes 4

360g chapati flour (*atta*) or plain wholewheat flour, plus extra for kneading and rolling out
2 teaspoons fine sea salt or table salt
about 250ml water, as needed
60g ghee or butter, melted, optional

Stir the chapati flour and salt together in a bowl. Add about 200ml of the water and mix until smooth. Slowly knead in enough of the remaining water to make a soft dough that isn't too sticky. The exact amount of water you will need depends on the absorbency of the flour you are using. Add it gradually – you might need a little more or a little less than specified here. Cover with a damp tea towel and leave to rest for 15 minutes.

Turn out the dough on a floured work surface and knead for a few minutes until smooth and elastic. With floured hands, divide the dough into 4 equal pieces and shape into balls. Flatten each ball between the palms of your hands, then, using a floured rolling pin, roll each into a 12cm disc. After each is rolled, gently slap it back and forth between your hands to remove the excess flour.

Heat 1 or 2 large *tawas* or frying pans over a high heat. Add as many chapatis as will fit and cook for 2 minutes, or until they start to dry out, bubble on the surface and there are brown spots on the bottoms. Turn the chapatis over and cook on the other side for 1–2 minutes until both sides are speckled brown. While the chapati are cooking, use a folded tea towel to press around the edge, so it bubbles up in the centre, creating a lighter texture. This also helps them cook more evenly.

Transfer to a tray or plate and brush with ghee or butter, if using. Cover with a tea towel and keep hot until all the breads are cooked.

Parathas

Parathas are a richer, flakier version of chapatis that are made by brushing the dough with melted ghee and folding several times before rolling it into various shapes. In the Punjab and North India, where I am from, they are usually triangular or round, whereas those made in Uttar Pradesh, for example, are more often square.

Makes 4

360g chapati flour (*atta*) or plain wholewheat flour, plus extra for kneading and rolling out
2 teaspoons fine sea salt or table salt
about 250ml water, as needed
90g ghee or butter, melted, optional

Prepare the dough as for the chapatis (page 288), and roll it into four 12cm discs. Working with 1 disc at a time, lightly brush ghee on top and sprinkle with a little flour, then fold in half. Apply another thin layer of ghee and sprinkle with more flour, then fold in half again to form a triangle. Press the layers together firmly, then roll out using the floured rolling pin, maintaining the shape. Repeat until all the parathas are shaped.

Heat 1 or 2 large *tawas* or frying pans over a medium heat. Add a paratha and cook for 2 minutes, or until it starts to dry out and there are brown spots on the bottom. Turn it over and cook on the other side for 1–2 minutes until both sides are speckled brown.

Increase the heat to high. Brush the paratha with melted ghee, flip it over and cook the other side for 30 seconds. Brush the new top surface with ghee, then flip the paratha and cook for a final 30 seconds. These are best served straight from the pan, or you can wrap them in a tea towel as they're ready and keep warm until all are cooked.

Onion & Spice Flatbreads

koki

Koki is a Sindhi bread made with chapati (*atta*) flour – similar to wholemeal flour – and flavoured with onions, mango powder, ajwain seeds, ground coriander and red chilli powder. You can find endless recipes for this bread, but this simple version works best for me. Serve these with a chutney (page 93), mint raita (page 292), plain yogurt or brushed with extra ghee.

Makes 14–16

500g chapati flour (*atta*) or plain wholemeal flour, plus extra for dusting
1 fresh red chilli, finely chopped
1 onion, finely chopped
2 tablespoons ghee, melted and cooled
1 tablespoon chopped coriander leaves
1 tablespoon ground coriander
2 teaspoons mango powder (*amchur*) or lemon juice
½ teaspoon ajwain seeds
½ teaspoon red chilli powder
a pinch of asafoetida
sea salt
200–325ml water, as needed
vegetable oil, for frying the breads

To make the dough, stir all the ingredients, except the water and vegetable oil, together in a large bowl with a pinch of salt. Make a well in the centre and slowly stir in 200ml water to make a soft dough that holds together. You might need up to an extra 125ml, depending on the absorbency of the flour, so add it tablespoon by tablespoon without letting the dough become too soft. Cover the dough with a tea towel and leave to rest for 30 minutes.

With floured hands, divide the dough into 14–16 equal balls, 60–70g each. Using a floured rolling pin, roll out each ball on a floured surface into a circle, 8–9cm across and 0.5cm thick.

Heat a large *tawa* or frying pan, ideally non-stick, over a medium-high heat until very hot. One at a time, slap a dough circle on to the pan and dry-fry for 1 minute, or until brown specks appear on the underside. Flip it over, press down the edge with a tea towel and repeat. Brush the top with vegetable oil, turn over and continue cooking for a further minute, or until the bread is light brown. These are best served straight from the pan, but you can transfer to a tray or plate lined with kitchen paper, cover with a tea towel and keep hot until all the breads are cooked.

Peanut
Dipping Sauce

Makes 400ml

150g skinned salted peanuts
60g dried red chillies, soaked
   in boiling water to cover for
   at least 20 minutes
1cm piece of fresh ginger,
   peeled and chopped
1 garlic clove, peeled
1 lemongrass stalk, outer layers
   removed and the stalk bashed
   and coarsely chopped
½ shallot, roughly chopped
3 tablespoons sunflower oil
2½ tablespoons tamarind
   extract (see Atul's tip,
   page 167)
1¾ tablespoons palm sugar
   or light brown sugar
¾ teaspoon sea salt
250ml water
150ml coconut milk
1 tablespoon sweet soy sauce
   (*kecap manis*)

Put the peanuts in a food processor and process until coarsely ground. Remove and set aside.

When the chillies are rehydrated, drain them and remove the stem ends. I like the heat the seeds give this sauce, but if you want a milder version go ahead and remove the seeds. Chop the chillies and add them to the food processor with the ginger, garlic, lemongrass and shallot, and process until a fine paste forms, scraping down the side of the bowl as necessary, and adding a little of the oil to help break down the ingredients into a finer paste.

Heat a wok over a high heat. Add the remaining oil and swirl around. Reduce the heat to medium, add the paste and stir-fry for a couple of minutes to cook the garlic and shallot. It should be smelling fragrant. Stir in the tamarind extract, sugar and salt, and continue stir-frying for 5 minutes or until the paste turns darker and the fat separates. You really have to keep your eyes on the wok at this point and keep stirring so nothing catches and burns.

Stir in the water, coconut milk, soy sauce and chopped peanuts, reduce the heat slightly and simmer, stirring often, for 10 minutes or until the sauce is thicker. Taste and adjust the salt, if necessary. Transfer to a bowl and set aside until required, or leave to chill completely and put in the fridge, where it will keep in a covered container in the fridge for up to 3 days.

Mint Raita

Serves 4

200g Greek yogurt
1 tablespoon finely chopped
　　mint leaves, plus a few extra,
　　to garnish
1 tablespoon ground toasted
　　cumin seeds (page 270)
sea salt

Mix together the yogurt, mint, ground cumin seeds and salt to taste. Cover and chill for up to 6 hours before serving. It will need a good stir before serving.

Tomato Salsa

This is a versatile chutney that can be served alongside many snacks and cold meats, or used as a dip. My twist on an otherwise traditional recipe is that I start by grilling the tomatoes, so the slightly charred skins add an umami flavour. Alternatively, grill the tomatoes over glowing coals on a barbecue for an added hint of smokiness.

Serves 6–8 as a side dish

10 garlic cloves, unpeeled
8 medium tomatoes
2 long, thin green chillies
100g coriander leaves
1 teaspoon prepared English
　　mustard
1¼ teaspoons finely ground
　　toasted cumin seeds
　　(page 270)
2 tablespoons freshly squeezed
　　lemon juice
2 tablespoons rapeseed oil
sea salt

Preheat the grill to medium-high. Place the garlic cloves and tomatoes in the grill pan and grill, turning occasionally, until both are lightly charred. When the garlic cloves are cool enough to handle, peel them.

Put the grilled garlic and tomatoes on a cutting board with the chillies, coriander leaves, mustard, ground cumin seeds and a pinch of salt, and chop together. You want a coarse texture with the charred skin incorporated. Transfer the mixture to a bowl. Stir in the lemon juice and rapeseed oil, taste and adjust the salt, if necessary. Keep any leftovers in a covered container in the fridge up to 3 days.

Mint Chutney

Available from Indian food shops and some large supermarkets, chaat masala is a powdered spice blend of asafoetida, mango powder (*amchur*), ground dried mint and black salt, mostly used as a salad seasoning. It has a tangy flavour.

Makes about 300g

200g mint leaves
100g coriander leaves
3 tablespoons freshly squeezed lemon juice
1 long, thin green chilli, stem removed
1 tablespoon finely chopped peeled fresh ginger
5 tablespoons Greek yogurt
1 tablespoon chaat masala
½ teaspoon red chilli powder
½ teaspoon salt, or to taste

Put the mint leaves, coriander leaves, lemon juice, chilli and ginger in a food processor, and process until a smooth paste forms. Transfer to a bowl. Stir in the yogurt, chaat masala, chilli powder and salt. Cover and chill for up to 1 day.

Yogurt & Mustard Seed Chutney

Makes about 300g

300g natural full-fat yogurt
1 tablespoon runny honey
1 tablespoon finely chopped mint leaves
1cm piece of fresh ginger, peeled and finely chopped
1 teaspoon sea salt
2 teaspoons sunflower oil
½ teaspoon black mustard seeds
¼ teaspoon turmeric
¼ teaspoon freshly squeezed lime juice, optional

This is best made as close as possible to serving, but it can be kept in a covered container in the fridge for up to 8 hours. Whisk the yogurt, honey, mint, ginger and salt together and set aside.

Heat the oil in a frying pan over a medium-high heat. Add the mustard seeds and turmeric and stir-fry until the seeds crackle and pop. Stir into the yogurt mixture. The sharpness of the yogurt can be adjusted with the lime juice, if you like. Leave to cool completely, then cover and chill until required. Give it a good stir just before serving.

Conversion Tables

Weights

metric	imperial
15g	½oz
20g	¾oz
30g	1oz
55g	2oz
85g	3oz
110g	4oz / ¼lb
140g	5oz
170g	6oz
200g	7oz
225g	8oz / ½lb
255g	9oz
285g	10oz
310g	11oz
340g	12oz / ¾lb
370g	13oz
400g	14oz
425g	15oz
450g	16oz / 1lb
1kg	2lb 4oz
1.5kg	3lb 5oz

Liquids

metric	imperial
5ml	1 teaspoon
15ml	1 tablespoon or ½fl oz
30ml	2 tablespoons or 1fl oz
150ml	¼ pint or 5fl oz
290ml	½ pint or 10fl oz
425ml	¾ pint or 16fl oz
570ml	1 pint or 20fl oz
1 litre	1¾ pints
1.2 litres	2 pints

Length

metric	imperial
5mm	¼in
1cm	½in
2cm	¾in
2.5cm	1in
5cm	2in
10cm	4in
15cm	6in
20cm	8in
30cm	12in

Useful conversions

1 tablespoon	= 3 teaspoons
1 level tablespoon	= approx. 15g or ½oz
1 heaped tablespoon	= approx. 30g or 1oz
1 egg	= 55ml / 55g / 1fl oz

Oven temperatures

°C	°C Fan	Gas Mark	°F
110°C	90°C Fan	Gas Mark ¼	225°F
120°C	100°C Fan	Gas Mark ½	250°F
140°C	120°C Fan	Gas Mark 1	275°F
150°C	130°C Fan	Gas Mark 2	300°F
160°C	140°C Fan	Gas Mark 3	325°F
180°C	160°C Fan	Gas Mark 4	350°F
190°C	170°C Fan	Gas Mark 5	375°F
200°C	180°C Fan	Gas Mark 6	400°F
220°C	200°C Fan	Gas Mark 7	425°F
230°C	210°C Fan	Gas Mark 8	450°F
240°C	220°C Fan	Gas Mark 9	475°F

index

Acknowledgements

Thank you to the entire team who has worked on this book – Jon, Meg, Emily, Beverly, Susanna, Mike, Anika and Vipin Krishnan, my Sous Chef at Vaasu. Thank you all for your work in bringing this book together in time; you always keep me on track and I'm grateful. I look forward to cooking for you from the book to celebrate our achievement.

An especially big thumbs up and shout out to Anika for the beautiful layout and illustrations. And a heartfelt thanks to Mike Cooper for always keeping up with the fierce speed of cooking on the food photography shoots – you're a superstar and always there to help.

Thank you to Melanie Childs for the PR, and Martine Carter, who helped me get the book together.

This wouldn't be possible without my entire kitchen brigade, who quietly allowed me to cook alongside them while I tested these recipes, and the team at Hawkyns for assisting in the shoot.

About the Author

Atul Kochhar's inimitable talent as a twice-Michelin-starred chef has changed the way people perceive and experience Indian food. He has been at the forefront of the Indian culinary industry for the over 25 years, and, inspired by his native India, Atul combines his heritage with his love of British ingredients to create and delivers modern Indian cuisine.

Atul's restaurant portfolio has grown from strength to strength, and in recent years he has opened a number of restaurants across the UK, including Sindhu, Hawkyns, Kanishka, Vaasu, Masalchi and Riwaz, as well as SAGA in Delhi, India.

Atul has written a number of successful books, including *Atul's Curries of the World, 30 Minute Curries* and *Fish, Indian Style,* and often appears at festivals across the UK.

He is the recognisable face of modern Indian cuisine on British television, regularly appearing on *Great British Menu, Saturday Kitchen* and *James Martin's Saturday Morning.* Most recently Atul's entrepreneurial nature made him the perfect investor on BBC2 and Netflix series, *Million Pound Menu.*

BLOOMSBURY ABSOLUTE
Bloomsbury Publishing Plc
50 Bedford Square, London, WC1B 3DP, UK
29 Earlsfort Terrace, Dublin 2, Ireland

BLOOMSBURY, BLOOMSBURY ABSOLUTE, the Diana logo and the
Absolute Press logo are trademarks of Bloomsbury Publishing Plc.

First published in Great Britain 2022

A catalogue record for this book is available from the British Library.
Library of Congress Cataloguing-in-Publication data has been
applied for.

ISBN: 9781472985996
ePUB: 9781472986009
ePDF: 9781472985989

2 4 6 8 10 9 7 5 3 1
Printed and bound in Italy by L.E.G.O. S.p.A.

To find out more about our authors and books visit www.bloomsbury.
com and sign up for our newsletters.

Publisher
Jon Croft

Commissioning Editor
Meg Boas

Senior Editor
Emily North

Art Director and Designer
Anika Schulze

Photographer
Mike Cooper

Photographer's Assistant
Ben Allen

Editor
Beverly LeBlanc

Home Economist
Susanna Tee

Proofreader
Susan Low

Indexer
Zoe Ross